Better Homes and Ga

bathroom decorating ideas under $100

Meredith® Books
Des Moines, Iowa

Bathroom Decorating Ideas Under $100

Contributing Project Manager/Writer: Jean Schissel Norman
Contributing Graphic Designer: Matthew Eberhart, Evil Eye Design, Inc.
Copy Chief: Terri Fredrickson
Publishing Operations Manager: Karen Schirm
Senior Editor, Asset and Information Management: Phillip Morgan
Edit and Design Production Coordinator: Mary Lee Gavin
Editorial Assistant: Kaye Chabot
Book Production Managers: Pam Kvitne, Marjorie J. Schenkelberg, Rick von Holdt, Mark Weaver
Contributing Copy Editor: Kelly Roberson
Contributing Proofreaders: Jeanette Astor, Julie Collins, Sara Henderson
Contributing Cover Photographer: King Au
Contributing Indexer: Stephanie Reymann

Meredith® Books

Executive Director, Editorial: Gregory H. Kayko
Executive Director, Design: Matt Strelecki
Managing Editor: Amy Tincher-Durik
Senior Editor/Group Manager: Vicki Leigh Ingham
Marketing Product Manager: Steve Rogers

Publisher and Editor in Chief: James D. Blume
Editorial Director: Linda Raglan Cunningham
Executive Director, Marketing: Steve Malone
Executive Director, New Business Development: Todd M. Davis
Executive Director, Sales: Ken Zagor
Director, Operations: George A. Susral
Director, Production: Douglas M. Johnston
Director, Marketing: Amy Nichols
Business Director: Jim Leonard

Vice President and General Manager: Douglas J. Guendel

Better Homes and Gardens® Magazine

Deputy Editor, Home Design: Oma Blaise Ford

Meredith Publishing Group

President: Jack Griffin
Executive Vice President: Bob Mate

Meredith Corporation

Chairman and Chief Executive Officer: William T. Kerr
President and Chief Operating Officer: Stephen M. Lacy

In Memoriam: E.T. Meredith III (1933–2003)

All of us at Meredith® Books are dedicated to providing you with information
and ideas to enhance your home. We welcome your comments and suggestions.
Write to us at: Meredith Books, Home Decorating and Design Editorial Department,
1716 Locust St., Des Moines, IA 50309-3023.

Introduction

Bathrooms—small but mighty—take more abuse per square foot than any other room in the house. Consider the facts. They're open 24/7, flooded with water, steamed by humidity, and jostled every which way due to the constant ebb and flow of family traffic. Is it any wonder they demand some attention every now and then?

Here's help. *Bathroom Decorating Ideas Under $100* includes page after page of bathroom ideas and fun makeover projects. The book, divided into nine style chapters, is paced so it's easy to pick the look that fits. Check out each chapter's tips, ideas, and projects guaranteed to work, whether the makeover costs considerably less than $100 or several multiples of $100.

Looking for bathroom designs? Visit the whole bathrooms that lead off each chapter in "5 ideas under $100."

Want to create a specific look? Read through the "Just a Little Splashier" pages for tips and products that deliver personal style.

Ready to roll up your sleeves and dig into design? Follow along with the step-by-step instructions in every chapter.

Need a quick idea to freshen up the bathroom before guests arrive? Look for the quick-and-easy ideas on every page, especially the tips labeled "Little Splashes."

Isn't it time to see just how far a $100 bill will stretch?

contents

6 romantic

Soak in the style of bathrooms designed just for grown-ups by adding elegant furnishings and fixtures wrapped around a soft color palette. Hang a chandelier, etch a mirror, or paint a lacy floor.

22 nature

Bring the feeling of woods and lakeshores into nature-inspired bathrooms by combining the rustic textures of wood and stone with serene shades of green. Add wood to a wall, frame botanicals, and plant a moisture-loving terrarium.

34 classic

Refresh dated bathrooms with a modern take on traditional style. Pour it on with two-color schemes and well-loved patterns, such as toile and florals. Skirt a damaged vanity, paint a toile-inspired floorcloth, and enhance a wall with a plaster finish over a standard stencil.

48 whimsy

Dip into playful colors and graphic shapes to revitalize boring bathrooms filled with plain white tile and fixtures. It's a look that suits everyone in the family. Add bold flowers to the walls, paint cabinet knobs, top a window with a valance, and make cut-paper artwork.

62 flea market

Decorate bathrooms with one-of-a kind style by filling them with flea market collections. Repurpose everything from barkcloth curtains to flower pots, hang plates as art, make a no-sew shade, and paint the walls with colorful stripes.

74 spa

Wash bathrooms with serenity by patterning them after a favorite spa. Build the look using the comfort of soft textures, smooth wood finishes, and neutral colors. Gather an herb bouquet for the tub, use a curtain rod as a supersize towel rack, and fill an old cabinet with spa gear.

86 beach

Replay favorite vacation memories by filling bathrooms with the beach-inspired colors of sand and sea glass. Gather shell collections to use as accents, create a beach swag for a window, frame old photographs for a wainscot, and build a wavy shelf to hold grooming supplies.

100 country

Gather favorite country furnishings, finishes, and colors to make bathrooms feel downright homey and fresh as a daisy. Transform a table into a vanity, add an aged finish to cabinetry, hang curtains from hooks, and paint a checkered floor.

114 kids

Add splash to bathrooms designed for children by using bright colors, fun patterns, and water-resistant finishes that serve up style for years. Stencil a ducky border, stamp a vinyl floor, and make a shower liner that corrals bath toys.

roma

Bathrooms shared with kids and guests have to look good and **work hard**. In your own bathroom, however, you can express your most romantic nature. So layer on the charm with flowery fabrics and wall coverings, pretty furniture, sweet light fixtures, and filmy window coverings. Your dream bath is just a few projects away.

suite retreat

An oversize bathroom leaves plenty of space for romantic touches, but most of these ideas work in a small space too.

5 ideas under $100

1. White, cream, and khaki create a soft yet defined background that plays up the textures of wood floors, walls, and ceilings. A neutral color scheme offers timeless appeal and is a smart choice to keep a bathroom shared by two from becoming too sweet.

2. Add beaded board on the bathroom walls, and cap the tops of the panels with molding. Purchase the beaded board in tongue-and-groove pieces that slot together. If the bathroom requires too much beaded board to suit the budget, duplicate the look with a two-color paint treatment and a shelf 15 inches from the ceiling.

3. A cabinet with glass doors makes perfect sense if there's room. Freshen up an existing piece with a coat of white paint, or look for a worn and inexpensive cabinet to update. Even a glass-door cabinet hung on the wall will do. For added romance, line the shelves with pretty fabric, or staple wallpaper to the back of the cabinet behind the shelves. Store stacks of fluffy towels and glass canisters filled with soaps and lotions.

4. Purchase a fancy light fixture at a flea market, and then coat it with fresh white paint. A fixture that seems too gaudy in gold is perfect in a soft neutral. Use spray paint for a smooth finish, and hang the fixture outside while painting. For an unexpected flourish, wrap white tulle around the top of the fixture; just make sure the tulle doesn't touch the lightbulbs.

5. Soften the floor with pretty woven or hooked rugs near the bathtub and in front of the sink. Vintage hooked rugs cost less than $50 at most antiques malls. To create a romantic color scheme, buy the rug first, then pick paint colors to match. If a new rug has a pretty pattern but colors that are too strong, lay the rug outdoors under the hot summer sun. Check to see if any sun-fading has occurred after 8 hours of exposure. Monitor the bleaching until you have achieved a vintage look.

little splashes

Surround a plateglass mirror installed on the bathroom wall with molding. Cutting miters in trim requires woodworking skill. If you are unskilled, use molding that includes corner blocks butted up to boards with straight cuts.

not from scratch

Here's how to create a pretty bathroom when the ceramic wall and floor tile stays put.

5 ideas under $100

1 Find a color scheme in a collection of antique plates, such as the trio hanging on the back wall. Take the plate to the paint store to find a matching color or have one custom-made. Just don't be tempted to play it safe by picking white paint. Wallpaper offers a pricier option. For a bargain, shop local paint and wallpaper stores for sales and returns, or shop online to find discounts. Another option is to create the look of wallpaper with paint and stencils. Unlimited paint color choices make this a smart and affordable solution.

2 Transform old light fixtures by purchasing fabric-covered shades. Look for shades that clip onto lightbulbs, which can be used even with ceiling-mounted fixtures. To refurbish old or inexpensive shades with fabric that underscores the color scheme, wrap the shades in fabric, and glue ribbon or other narrow trims to the shades' bottom and top edges. Update a fixture's shabby finish by masking around the fixture and spray-painting it with a metallic paint that matches the bathroom faucet.

3 Wrap a new skirt around a dated sink to hide all that unsightly plumbing. Use hook-and-loop fastening tape (one side sticks to the sink and the other is sewn to the fabric) or use fabric or flexible adhesive material and adhesive-back hook-and-loop tape. Make sure to create a skirt that easily removes for laundering.

4 Store bathroom gear in style. Cover up a cabinet by replacing glass doors with metal screens, and hang shirred fabric in the doors from top to bottom. Fabric adds color, pattern, and softness while hiding the mess. Keep towels handy by stacking them in a vintage wicker plant stand. Its long, narrow shape makes it just the right size for a bathroom. Or add a peg rack to hold towels while they dry and clothing during bath time.

5 Relax on an upholstered chair. Move a pretty chair from anywhere else in the house into the bathroom. It won't cost a penny. Just imagine the luxury of having an elegant perch handy before or after a bath.

little splashes

▌ Paint the bathroom ceiling with a soft tint of a color used in the room. Try sky blue or soft lilac for romantic appeal.

translating french

A bathroom can work hard and look elegant too, especially when it's designed with French accents.

5 ideas under $100

① Frame the bathtub with bold beams, then paper the wall to create a focal point. Search out affordable wallpapers online. To create the look of a dramatic print when wallpaper is too expensive, use a stencil on one wall only.

② Lean a ladder against the wall as a surprising and movable towel rack. If there's worn paint on the ladder, brush on two coats of polyurethane to protect the surface of the ladder from water and the towels from stains. Drape towels over the rungs, hanging hand towels on the narrower upper rungs.

③ Update a plain vanity with a decorative finish. Paint the cabinet a base color, then cut out intricate flower and leaf paper pieces and adhere them to the center of the doors using a decoupage medium. For even more detail, use a small artist's brush and a freehand stroke to highlight the vanity details, such as around the recessed-panel doors. Rub an antiquing glaze over the surface, and use a soft absorbent cloth to remove some of the glaze for an aged look. Protect the decoupage and the finish with two coats of the decoupage medium.

④ Bring in furniture. A padded chair makes a great landing spot for reading material; it also adds a soft look to the bathroom. A three-shelf stand provides space for bathroom gear and is easy to move near the vanity or the bathtub. If there's plenty of space, move a tall cabinet or dresser into the bathroom to hold bathroom supplies and clothing.

⑤ Add hanging shelves for storage and display. Look for vintage shelves at flea markets, and feel free to paint them to fit your decor. Make sure to use wall anchors when hanging the shelves so they can hold the weight of the displayed items. Experts at your local home center or hardware store can give hanging advice depending on the weight of the shelf and the composition of the walls. To simplify leveling the hanging shelves, use a laser level that suctions to the wall and projects a level beam of light.

little splashes

❚ Don't give up on a favorite fabric for the bath because it requires drycleaning. To see if it will withstand washing, buy a half yard and wash it in the gentle cycle. If the colors stay true and shrinkage is minimal, it's good to sew.

just a little splashier

Think pretty when buying the elements for a romantic bathroom. Soft colors, sweet patterns, and elegant shapes build a look that's suited for two.

get the look

▐ Select bathroom colors from the lighter, clearer end of the spectrum. Look for clear pinks and lilacs, pale yellows, pastel blues and greens, and neutrals that take their cues from clear rather than muddy colors. Start the color search with a patterned plate or flowery fabric. Consider wallpaper as well as paint in favorite tones.

▐ Add objects that sparkle, such as mirrors in old-fashioned gold-leaf frames or elegant metal faucets and fittings. Look for curvy knobs in polished glass to update the vanity. Sparkle instantly casts a romantic glow.

▐ Gather blooms to toss on every surface, from wallpapered walls to hooked rugs. Make a spot for a single flower in a sweet glass vase.

▐ Soften the room with a slipcovered chair, a flouncy sink skirt, or a pleated window treatment. Add detail to plain fabrics with ribbon tied into bows to hang a curtain panel, beaded trim glued to the edge of a window shade, and buttons stitched to plump pillows.

▐ Top off the room and add a dramatic focal point with a sparkly chandelier that's slightly overscale for the space. Supplement its glow with wall-hung sconces that provide bright light for grooming.

▐ Add details that pamper, such as lace edging or monograms on towels and covered glass canisters filled with soaps and bath salts. Line drawers and open shelves with delicate scented papers. Scatter framed prints on the walls.

Ceramic tile Romance any bathroom with ceramic tile in whisper-soft colors. Pave the floor in a tiny bathroom with a subtle pattern of colors. In a larger space, add a backsplash above a pedestal sink, or use a row of tiles as a border.

Glass knobs Think of glass knobs as jewels for a plain vanity. They add flair in the same way jewelry dresses up a basic black dress. Splurge on only a few, or look for bargain knobs online by typing "affordable knobs" in a search engine.

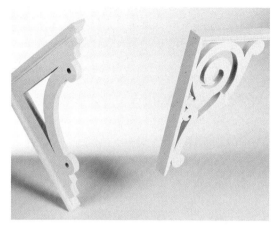

Shelf A simple shelf set on brackets spray-painted in shiny chrome looks all dressed up. The shelf provides a convenient spot for storing and displaying bath salts, soaps, and lotions.

Brackets Carved brackets, painted in a buttery shade, provide perches for custom-cut glass or wood shelves. For even more storage, hang several shelves on one wall.

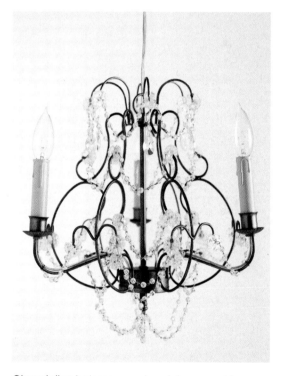

Hooked rug A room filled with hard surfaces, such as porcelain fixtures and ceramic tile, deserves a soft finish in the form of a flowery rug.

Chandelier A glamorous chandelier can add a romantic touch over a tub without a shower. If electrical wiring doesn't run to this spot, hang a chandelier outfitted with candles. A chandelier also might be a good style substitute for a standard bathroom ceiling light.

Fabric-covered boxes Store bathroom supplies out of sight in boxes wrapped in vintage-look fabric and tied with ribbons.

good reflections

Although it's required equipment in a bathroom, a mirror doesn't have to be dull. Here are two stylish options.

mirror monogram

Etching cream permanently makes its mark on new or old mirrors. Unlike stencils for paint, this stencil is cut from adhesive-back vinyl that temporarily protects the mirror surface from the etching cream.

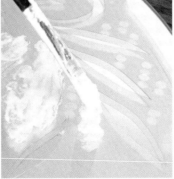

HOW TO
etch a mirror

1. **Trace** the stencil onto clear adhesive-back vinyl (leave the backing on).
2. **Pull away** a small portion of the vinyl's paper backing; position the vinyl on a clean mirror. Continue to pull away the backing paper, adhering the vinyl to the glass and working out any bubbles.
3. **Cut away** vinyl using a crafts knife along the traced lines to expose areas of the mirror that will be etched. Use the blade point to remove small pieces, *far left*.
4. **Cover** additional exposed mirror that won't be etched using extra vinyl.
5. **Read** the instructions for the etching cream (available at crafts stores) before beginning. Work in a well-ventilated area, and wear latex gloves for protection.
6. **Apply** the etching cream evenly and thickly to the mirror, *left*, with an artist's brush.
7. **Allow** the cream to set for the prescribed time or longer. Wash off the cream under running water following the manufacturer's instructions.

upsy-daisy mirror

Recycle an abandoned dresser mirror by hanging it upside down from a plate rail attached to the wall.

little splashes

▮ Install a dimmer to turn down the bathroom's light level for a relaxing soak in the tub. Replace wattage with a soft glow by tucking votive candles in etched glasses that perch on a nearby shelf.

▮ Hanging techniques vary with the mirror's structure and how it was originally attached to furniture. Here the "feet" of the mirror are notched so they fit snugly around the bottom of the plate rail. Drill and screw the legs to the plate rail's molding to secure the mirror. Fill screw holes with spackling compound, and sand smooth. Paint the mirror frame the same color as the rest of the woodwork for a unified look.

romantic details

Treat standard surfaces with lacy finishes using cutwork papers and paint.

crystal clear

A lamp can add a romantic touch to any bathroom. Here's how to work some magic on a dated or damaged lamp.

Start with a flea-market lamp base. Buy a self-adhesive lampshade kit, available at crafts and fabric stores, to fit the lamp base and follow the easy instructions to cover it with decorative paper. Or, for an existing shade, roll the shade over the reverse side of the decorative paper chosen to cover it, tracing along the top and bottom edges while moving the shade. Cut out the paper, adding ½ inch along the top and bottom edges. Test-fit the paper over the shade; cut the ends so they overlap 1 inch. Spray the back of the paper with spray adhesive, following the manufacturer's instructions. Center the paper on the shade and smooth it out, overlapping ends and folding the top and bottom edges to the shade's interior. To finish, hang chandelier crystals from holes pierced with a large needle through the shade's bottom edge.

lacy floor

A paper doily is the secret ingredient for this stenciled floor. Although the design looks delicate, it's protected with polyurethane so it will stand up to water and wear.

HOW TO

paint a lacy floor

1. **Measure** the floor and pencil squares based on the size of the doilies. On this floor doilies create a checkered pattern edged with a 6½-inch-wide striped border.
2. **Lay** doilies facedown on kraft paper; lightly spray with stencil adhesive from a crafts store. Dry until tacky. Place the doilies, tacky side down, on the floor, *far left*. Lay paper over each doily, and rub firmly.
3. **Tape** off the border using quick-release painter's tape.
4. **Use** a small foam roller to apply the paint. Dip the roller into water-base paint, and roll it several times on newspaper to blot some of the paint. Roll over the doily and the border.
5. **Let** paint dry to the touch; carefully remove the doilies using a razor blade, *near left*. Remove the painter's tape from the border; let paint dry for 24 hours.
6. **Seal** the painted surface and protect it from wear by applying two coats of polyurethane, sanding lightly between coats.

shabby to chic

Turn worn-out dressers and cabinets into stylish storage for the bathroom using paint and etching cream.

dress it up

Revitalize an old wood dresser with stripes painted in periwinkle and white. Touches of yellow highlight the details. To paint an old dresser, make sure any veneer is intact; attach any loose pieces with woodworker's glue. Sand the surface, coat with primer, and let dry. Sand lightly after each coat; remove dust using a tack cloth. Paint the base coat white; let dry. Add accents of yellow. Measure and mark the stripes using a colored pencil that closely matches the stripes. Mask the white stripes using painter's tape; paint blue using a narrow foam roller. Protect the finish with two coats of polyurethane.

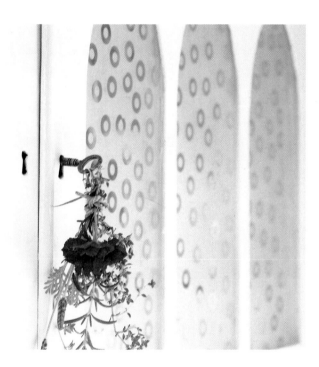

cabinet redo, inside and out

If the bathroom is too small for a freestanding piece of furniture, consider adding a vintage item that hangs on the wall and stores favorite things. For an inexpensive option, look for cabinets that need a good cleaning and a fresh coat of paint.

▌ This flea market cabinet was found with missing glass panes and wood veneer. A new coat of paint and etched replacement glass play up the delicate lines. (See the instructions for etching a mirror on page 16.) Drawers inside accommodate lavender, face cloths, and bath powder, while the shelf holds bottles of floral water and bars of soap. To hang the cabinet, drill through the back and into studs in the wall; screw through the cabinet into the wall.

natur

A room focused on water seems a fitting spot for nature-inspired decor. Gather the textures of the outdoors—rocks, wood, leaves, flowers, and moss—and mix them with the most soothing shades of green. In this hectic world, it's a treat to soak away worries in a bathroom that's almost as relaxing as a walk along a lake or through the woods.

water world

Create a private getaway that feels like a sauna built deep in the piney woods.

5 ideas under $100

1 Line a bathing nook with beautiful cedar planking that's suited to high-humidity areas. Leave the cedar boards unsealed and they'll release a woodsy scent when the bathroom fills with humidity. However, to preserve the natural color of the boards and prevent them from turning silvery gray, brush them with a wood sealer.

2 Pick the color palette from earthy tones, but add a little color punch as a surprise. That might mean choosing green—bold chartreuse or soft sage—to accent natural wood and slate. To give walls a personal touch, add a horizontal line in stripes of avocado and licorice using painter's tape and a carpenter's level. Paint the stripes and then remove the tape. Painter's tape goes on easily and pulls off without damaging paint.

3 Replace a standard sink with a sculptural pedestal one that reflects the calm, cool nature of this look. If you are unfamiliar with plumbing, trade jobs with a friend who knows how to install the sink. For a pedestal sink that costs less than $100, faucet included, search at a home center. Here, a bunk bed ladder stands in as a towel rack with the same cool and collected character as the sink.

4 Dress up a built-in cabinet or freestanding cupboard with bamboo inserts on the door panels. Remove the original panels and tack the bamboo inserts on the inside of the doors. Or cut a bamboo table runner to size and glue over a paneled door. Bamboo also offers a fitting treatment for bathroom windows; look for blinds at discount retailers and cut them to fit. Turn long bamboo sticks into art by tying twine around the center and standing them in a corner.

5 Add accessories, such as a rustic mirror, a narrow cedar shelf, a bathside table made from an upended woven basket, and a rattan bench. Varying textures, from smooth to rough and hard to soft, duplicates what happens in nature. The smooth stones on the tub wall are purchased votives. Gather large stones, a no-cost finishing touch, and tuck them under the edge of the clawfoot tub to serve as a reminder of a walk along a river's edge.

little splashes

▌ Stacks of pretty bath towels might be all the art a bathroom needs. Roll them up and stack them like logs on a bathroom shelf, or pile a few on a painted chair.

rustic and refined

A focal-point tub pairs with paneled wood walls to create this backwoods beauty.

5 ideas under $100

① Wood paneling sets the scene for rustic style. For a sophisticated yet woodsy look, select wide wood pieces with a smooth finish that
② can be sealed with two coats of polyurethane. Romance the space with wallpaper applied above the wood paneling.

A shelf all around the room makes space for votive candles and other narrow accessories. Screw the shelves to wood or metal brackets spaced every 24 inches. Place the shelf around the room to create a strong horizontal line that stays clear of water spray.

③ Soft green paint revives an old vanity and provides pleasing contrast to the room's wood tones. To pick green paint that suits a nature theme, opt for shaded or grayed colors rather than the bright greens of spring. Most manufacturers separate their colors by brights or shades to ease the selection process. When a room is filled with wood, select a lighter color for the accents to keep the room looking fresh.

④ Airy curtains and a floral rug add pampering accents that soften the look and feel of the space. Sheer curtains allow light into the space while screening the view. Purchase a yard or two of sheer fabric to cover the bottom half of a double-hung window. Search for a rug that stands up to moisture, supports the color scheme, and fills the space. If a floral rug is hard to find, look for a patterned rug in soft shades of green.

⑤ Nothing adds a sense of nature as quickly as elements pulled from the outdoors. For flowers, pick delicately scented blooms in pastel shades. Stick to a one-color palette so the flowers blend in rather than stand out. Place them by the sink in pitchers or vases, or add a few in tiny bottles that sit on the shelves. To fill in between blooms, slip long-lasting leaves into vases; leaves last for months in water. Or opt for branches to reflect the seasons: just-budding leaves in spring, green leaves in summer, colorful leaves in fall, and bare branches in winter.

little splashes

▌ Make a custom rug by sewing standard bath mats or small rugs together. Combine them end-to-end for a runner or side-to-side to make a rectangular floor mat. Wait to buy the bathmats when they go on sale.

just a little splashier

Ready to start shopping? Gathering supplies might not be the same as a walk in the woods, but a similar sense of discovery should guide any purchases. Search for natural textures and colors to bring this look to life.

get the look

▮ Gather paint cards filled with every shade of green; it's the perfect color to play off natural wood and stone. Sort through the colors, selecting light, medium, and dark tones as well as a variety of hues from yellow-green to blue-green.

▮ Wood rules in a bathroom inspired by nature. Consider the reddish tones of maple and the yellow tones of oak; use them both in the same room. Check out wood options in paneling, vanities, flooring, and furniture too.

▮ Opt for metal tones that complement the wood colors. Copper might add a glow, while brushed nickel can seem cold. To make the choice, place the metal against a variety of woods, and note which combination looks best together.

▮ Keep a nature-inspired bathroom from looking too much like a woodsy cabin by adding elements such as leafy wallpaper, delicate glass, and dressy knobs. Play curvy faucets against stone or wood countertops. Edge a shimmery mirror with textured twigs. Line etched glass canisters on a wood shelf.

▮ Refine the look with fabrics and fibers. Rustic burlap edged with sisal braid or fringe looks good as Roman shades or curtain panels. Sisal rugs soften stone-look vinyl tiles, while hooked rugs in floral patterns provide even more comfort.

▮ Accentuate nature's style with accessories. Consider framing and hanging pressed leaves in groupings, or gluing stones to the ends of curtain rods as fresh-from-the-forest finials.

Paint Green, from light to dark and bright to grayed, offers the perfect background color for a nature-inspired bathroom. To use several shades of green in one bathroom, select a light, midtone, and darker color from one paint card.

Plants For an easy-care plant that adds natural green to the bathroom, consider the ZZ plant, short for *Zamioculcas zamiifolia*. It tolerates dim interior light and neglect, is impervious to pests, and doesn't fuss over its watering schedule. In fact, the only way to kill it is by overwatering.

Floor paint Go green on the bathroom floor with a fresh coat of paint. Try one of the new high-performance floor enamels that offer lots of color options, dry quickly, and resist wear.

Scented candles Aroma is part of the woodland experience. Bring those natural scents home and change the mood instantly with a variety of aromatic candles. Make sure each person who uses the bath selects a scent that suits.

Accessories Collect elements that repeat nature's textures—stone votives, a hand-carved wood bowl, and a rustic brush. Little touches like this add a bit of nature's style to a standard bathroom.

Rain showerhead Shower under an oversize showerhead for the feel of falling rain. It's okay if it isn't the real thing. Search local home centers and the Internet for options.

Botanical prints Vintage prints can be pricey, but never fear. Look for inexpensive prints on the Internet, or photocopy copyright-free material from vintage books. To give the new prints an aged look, lightly wipe them with brewed tea; let dry. Frame several prints to create a focal point on a wall.

fresh picks

Choose botanical accents—modern black-and-white flower photographs, vintage framed pressed flowers, or a dramatic tile backsplash—to complement the room.

be inspired

This dramatic tile mural over the bathroom sink, *below,* tops $100, but it's possible to create a similar look by framing a botanical print under glass. If a mirror is needed in the location, suspend a frameless mirror from the botanical's frame edge, and hang it over the botanical print.

photo finishing

Small black-and-white photos surrounded by oversize white mats and frames, *above,* offer a fresh take on the framed botanical and add a modern touch to a nature-inspired bathroom. For an inexpensive option, frame black-and-white greeting cards, photocopy colored cards in sepia, or shoot photographs. Use a digital camera to capture blooms in a home garden or a public garden. Load the photos on a computer, then crop them to create an interesting composition. Print and frame. Look for affordable frames on the sale shelves of local crafts stores, or shop online. Add in the cost of shipping before buying.

rings around the tub

Framed botanicals march in double file around the bathroom walls, *opposite.* Use photocopies from a book of botanicals so there's no need to worry about moisture damage to valuable prints. Choose matching frames for the most drama.

outside in

Soft colors and strong textures perfectly blend with nature. For inspiration, think bark and leaves, rocks and water, and petals and stems.

fern floor cloth

Invite the outdoors in with natural fibers and from-the-forest forms and hues. A stenciled pattern on a bamboo mat adds graphic punch.

HOW TO

stencil a fern floor cloth

1. **Cut** two stencils of the same design from acetate or cardboard. Two stencils allow painting to continue without waiting for paint to dry on a single stencil.
2. **Test** the pattern before painting by arranging paper frond cutouts on the mat in a random pattern to make sure of the look.
3. **Replace** the cutouts with a stencil taped to the mat. Stencil the ferns in a medium-tone green acrylic paint using a stencil brush.
4. **Blot** the stencil brush on paper towels to remove excess paint; apply the paint using an up-and-down or pouncing motion. Less paint means sharper lines.
5. **Let** the stencil patterns dry. Brush on two coats of polyurethane to protect the painted ferns from bath splashes.

little splashes

A walk in the woods can deliver the raw materials for a seasonal update: smooth stones to fill a bowl, small branches to slip into a glass cylinder, and handfuls of moss to heap in a rustic compote.

pot it up

Plants love the high humidity of a bathroom, *above*. In return, they add fresh smells and bright colors to the space. Take plants from the garden at the end of the growing season, or pot them up fresh for the bathroom. This collection of herbs—basil, curly parsley, oregano, and rosemary—offers stimulating scents as well as fresh ingredients for dinner, but any aromatic plant will scent the space.

bottle garden

A deep windowsill or small bathroom table provides the setting for a bottle garden, *above*. Search for green glass at a flea market. Most pieces cost $10 or less. The glass looks beautiful and dramatic when gathered in a collection and complements fresh-picked flowers. For added interest, wrap bottles with wire or raffia.

moss and rocks

Preserve souvenirs from a walk in the woods by placing them in a glass compote that sits by the bathroom window, *left*. The steam from daily showers and a spritz of water will keep the moss healthy and green. Nestle pinecones alongside the moss for a woodsy composition.

class

Classic style gets fresh in the bathroom with two-tone color palettes, traditional floral and toile patterns, and elegant details. Look for accessories that feature classic motifs, such as a Chippendale chair back and wide molding around a mirror. Dressmaker's details add good looks to soft gear such as shower curtains and sink skirts. Tradition reigns in the bath.

simply put

Details such as a toile-skirted sink and crisp shutters turn a ho-hum bathroom into a classic sanctuary.

5 ideas under $100

1 Play up the best details of a bathroom. If the room comes with a classic black-and-white tile floor or vintage tile on the walls, pick one strong color as an accent and give every other surface a coat of white paint. Make sure the white paint blends with the white of the tile. If the paint is a lot whiter than the tile, it will make the tile look dingy. Freshen up towel bars with black enamel.

2 Skirt the sink with classic lines and hide an out-of-date vanity at the same time. For easy access to the cabinet storage, remove the doors and design the skirt so that it overlaps in the front. For a removable skirt, add tiny cup hooks along the top edge of the vanity and grommets along the top edge of the skirt. Align the hooks and grommets so the skirt wraps smoothly around the vanity. Outfit the vanity with pull-out metal baskets.

3 Replace window treatments with crisp white shutters. Vinyl shutters cost less than wood ones and stand up to the humidity of a bathroom without warping. Check online or at a local home center for options.

4 Make a light cover for a tired, over-the-sink fluorescent fixture by cutting wood to length, adding a molding rosette to each end, and attaching the cover to the wall using L brackets. Make sure the cover extends at least 2 inches beyond the bulb. A simple solution like this is perfect for a rental apartment. Consider replacing a tired fluorescent fixture with a double-light fixture to add needed light. Match the metal of the fixture to the metal of the faucet for a consistent look.

5 Use accessories to add personality to the bath. To create drama in a small bathroom, look for bold accessories rather than many small things. Mirrors and oversize letters pair up to spell TOE on the wall, *right.* Collect both mirrors and letters at flea markets, and hang them together. Mirrors make a space seem larger by bouncing light around and reflecting the opposite walls.

little splashes

▮▮ Eliminate clutter that can make a small bathroom feel cramped. Slip bath gear inside baskets, totes, and cabinets. If there isn't enough storage in the bathroom, adopt a hallway closet for stashing extra towels and bulky supplies.

awash in pattern

Toile, a traditional motif, makes a style statement as it wraps from walls and curtains to rug. How classic!

5 ideas under $100

1 Large patterns might seem overwhelming for a standard-size bathroom, but a two-color toile can bring it all together. Use just one pattern and color combination for the best effect, and spread it around as wallpaper, window covering, shower curtain, and rug. Repetition of a large-scale pattern turns it into the background rather than the focal point.

2 Ground the red-and-white color scheme with a generous helping of black. Black steps in with white as bold tiles for the floor, *left*. The graphic checked pattern provides a modern combination with toile. Look for vinyl tiles for less

3 than $3 a tile. The easiest option is to use self-adhesive tiles over a smooth but worn floor; the backing peels off to reveal a sticky surface.

Chunks of solid color contrast with the busy toile pattern. Use a wall of plain white tile, a solid lining for the shower curtain, or bold towels to provide pattern relief.

4 Good-looking details add up. An open shelf with a decorative top provides resting spots for plants and gear. Other ideas that yield a big impact include cording along the edge of curtain tiebacks, decorative pottery that sits on the floor, and a sink skirted in a companion fabric.

5 Craft a classic rug by simplifying some of the toile designs and transferring them to a floor cloth. The easiest way to make a floor cloth is to cut the shape from a remnant of vinyl flooring. Turn the flooring to the reverse side, and prime it. Enlarge the toile patterns and transfer them to the flooring; paint. Add a bold border to help the rug stand in relief to the floor. The large-scale toile pattern flows from the edges of the floor cloth toward the center so the rug can be enjoyed from any direction. Two coats of polyurethane protect the design. For a ready-to-stencil toile pattern, try an online search engine.

little splashes

Gather up vintage glasses, either etched or colored, for votive holders that mix but don't match. Line them up on a narrow shelf.

small and stylish

Even a tiny guest bathroom offers space for style and character. Here's how to add them both using vintage details.

5 ideas under $100

1. Create a neutral background so a small space feels larger. A neutral space doesn't mean just one color, however. Shades of creamy and pure whites help blend the various colors of bathroom fixtures. This technique also creates more interest than using just one color. If starting with a wood wall, consider coating it with a creamy glaze that adds color and still lets the texture of the wood show through.

2. Pick an unforgettable mirror. This Gothic-style version adds style and provides enough mirror for grooming. Look for an old window to make into the project. Just remove the glass and paint the wood. A mirror shop can cut a mirror to fit the frame openings.

3. Stretch elegant shelving across a wall to hold charming objects and grooming supplies. This slice of marble sits on rustic brackets. For marble, check out precut door sills at your local home center. These narrow pieces work perfectly as shelves, just be sure to use sturdy brackets to support the marble.

4. Soften the space with a skirted sink. Make the skirt just like a piece of clothing by sewing a "waistband" around the top and tucking and sewing the fabric to make pleats. Use hook-and-loop fastening tape (one side sews to the skirt and the other sticks to the vanity) to secure the skirt in place. For easy access to the storage under the skirt, overlap two sections at the center front or side.

5. Add classic accents with accessories. Transfer lotions into pretty bottles or purchase bath salts in attractive containers perfect for display. Fill a pitcher with a classic flower such as larkspur, add metal accessories including a towel bar and sconces, and fill a lined basket with folded guest towels. Add monograms to fluffy white bath towels to make a style statement (check out the embroidery kiosk at a local shopping mall for this service). And don't forget to hang transferware plates on the wall to incorporate a favorite pattern and color.

little splashes

Keep favorite pieces of jewelry handy by hanging them as art near the bathroom vanity. Consider a row of delicate hooks to hold bracelets and necklaces.

just a little splashier

Whether searching online or in stores, look for classic shapes to ground your classic style. There's room for some surprises, but only when the basics are in place.

get the look

▋Search out traditional colors with a fresh kick to give classic style a modern attitude. That might mean opting for a brighter green or stronger blue, or combining colors in unexpected ways. Why not pair hot pink with taupe instead of using classic red with cream?

▋Gather up classic patterns in fabrics, wallpapers, and stencils. Look for toiles, florals, checks, and stripes. Experiment with combinations, such as combining a bold stripe with a floral or using an oversize check with a miniature toile print. The idea is to try something new.

▋Soften the bathroom with fabrics made into tailored Roman shades for the windows or a pleated skirt around the sink vanity.

▋Select new surfaces from classic materials, such as marble, plaster, beaded board, wood, ceramic tile, porcelain, and intricate metal. If these surfaces are too expensive, duplicate the style with look-alike products or painted finishes.

▋Make the biggest splash on the room's focal point. If it's the floor, use wood flooring or strip the floor back to wood. If the focus is on the vanity, price how much a marble top will cost. Look for marble remnants at substantial savings.

▋Finish the room with accessories, such as framed prints gathered on one wall, antique shelves to showcase collections or provide storage, and an oversize vintage frame outfitted with a new mirror to hang over the vanity.

Wallpaper Use wallpaper—especially in a small bath—to warm up the space, add pattern and color, and set a classic mood. Choose toile in subtle khaki and cream or a floral pattern that features a range of soft tones.

Light fixture Shed a little light and style on a bathroom with an elegant fixture. If replacing a single-bulb sconce, consider a triple-sconce fixture that delivers a flood of light without a wiring change. Shiny chrome complements classic style.

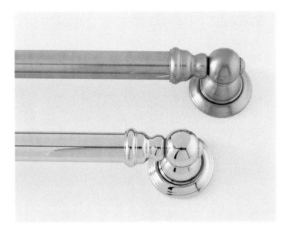

Towel bars Select from classic metals such as shiny chrome or burnished brass. Match the metals to faucets and knobs for consistency.

Peg rack Keep clutter under control by adding peg racks to the bathroom. Select a premade rack with decorative details and glass knobs for holders. Or make one using decorative trim and delicate knobs from the home center.

Mirror Gold might seem too formal for some styles, but it sets the right tone for a classic bathroom. Go all out by picking a mirror with a lot of detail. Look for elegant frames at flea markets, and then gild them with gold leaf or brush-on paint that includes real metal particles that tarnish over time.

Ceramic tile Patterns appear on more than wallpaper. Consider elegant embossed tile for a sophisticated wall treatment. To keep costs down, use just a few tiles as a border or backsplash.

Chippendale chair If there's room, squeeze a chair with a classic pedigree into the bathroom. For a surprising touch, unscrew the upholstered seat, wrap it with terry cloth, and reattach it.

classic walls

Artistry on the walls can turn these flat planes into the focal point of the room. Consider stenciling with plaster or adding stripes with paint.

plaster stencils

Decorative finishing transforms ordinary drywall into a one-of-a-kind wall finish.

HOW TO
stencil with plaster

1. **Coat** walls with oil-base primer; let dry. For products for this wall finish, check out paint stores or home centers.
2. **Roll** a medium coat of stone finish onto the surface using a special fabric roller, leaving thick and thin patches of texture. Let set for 10 minutes. Knock down any peaks with a stainless-steel trowel.
3. **Position** stencil and, using a plastic taping knife, apply a plaster material over the stencil openings. Vary the thickness of the plaster material to create a broken-plaster effect. Remove the stencil, *below left*; let dry.
4. **Sand** rough edges with 220-grit sandpaper; dust off. Fill any gaps in the design by skip-troweling the plaster material onto the surface in a medium thickness, *below center.*
5. **Create** two or three glaze mixtures by tinting the glazes. Mist the surface with a light film of water. Brush on the glazes and blend them into the plaster materials using a synthetic stippling brush. Allow the colors to stay darker in some areas. Blot with a dry terry-cloth towel, *below right,* and dry-brush with a soft-bristle brush.

subtle stripes

These stripes may look like wallpaper, but they're
not. The effect is achieved by coating the wall with
a base of buttercream paint, then painting stripes
in a soft taupe. These similar shades offer subtle
contrast that supports a traditional look. To create
the stripes, mask off vertical lines using painter's
tape; burnish the tape edges to keep paint from
bleeding underneath. Paint the stripes with a lightly-
filled brush to create a textured effect that mimics
the look of fabric.

little splashes

▊ For a seamless appearance between the
tub and wall, tint caulk to match the tub and
ceramic tile. Look for custom caulking at a
home center or hardware store.

soft by design

*A bathroom seems far from cold and clinical when yards
of fabric soften the surfaces. Here's how to make it work.*

dressing in style

A dressing table filled with favorites makes starting
the day a little more enjoyable. Create these projects
from scratch, or add extra details to purchased
items. For the table, add a pleated top using floral
fabric over a basic white skirt made from a sheet.
Top a bench cover with a monogrammed

handkerchief hand-stitched to the seat; bands of
checked fabric and buttons hold the corners in
place. A plain lampshade sports a new cover of
white pique cut on the bias. When gathered, the
shade creates a feminine flounce. Wrap the shade's
top with a gingham ribbon tied in a bow.

tub cover-up

Fabric can offer some surprising twists. In this elegant bathroom with a stand-alone shower, it's used to disguise the tub. (Look closely to spot the tub in the back corner.) A custom-made platform, draped in fabric, tops the tub and creates elegant seating. More fabric covers pillow forms and tops a vintage stool. Gather a variety of woven and printed fabrics in similar tones to create a classic look that's restful and serene.

whim

Turn a playful decorating style into a bathroom redo that's as much fun as splashing in the tub. It's easy to do by adding lighthearted details, such as edging a shower curtain with a row of ball fringe, hanging paper chandeliers over a soaking tub, or layering surfaces with painted flowers, dots, and stripes. Isn't it time to come in and play?

going dotty

A polka-dot theme gives this bathroom a bubbly personality.

5 ideas under $100

① Spread on some sunshine with a coat of lively yellow paint to create a backdrop for the polka-dot projects. If the bathroom fills with steam after showers, buy paint mixed with mildewcide to keep mold at bay.

② Embellish a tile mirror with porcelain or glass paints in the bathroom's colors. These special paints come in sizes as small as 2 ounces, and guarantee that hand-painted dots won't wash away. For this simple effect, use a paint pen to make circles and fill in the centers with porcelain or glass paint. To add dots to a painted wood frame, use acrylic crafts paints, also available in small bottles.

③ A playful dot motif dresses up a shower curtain. To make the curtain, sew two bath sheets together lengthwise. Following the manufacturer's instructions, attach 13 grommets 2 inches from the curtain top. Cut various-size circles from coordinating washcloths and adhere to the curtain with fabric glue. Stitch rickrack trim and ball fringe to the bottom of the shower curtain.

④ Replace dated sconces with modern versions to freshen a tired bath. Look for a wide selection of sconces that cost less than $100 at a local home center. Or use an online search engine and type in "discount light fixtures." If it's too pricey to replace existing sconces, look for replacement shades to give a bathroom just the lift it needs.

⑤ Buy a pile of towels and dress them up with trim. It's the quickest way to freshen a bath and an easy way to express personal style. Make sure to wash the trim and the towels before pairing them becausse one might shrink more than the other. Stitch the trim in place, or adhere it using fabric glue. Follow the directions on the glue to ensure the towels will stand up to a spin in the washer and a tumble in the dryer. While shopping, add a new towel bar to the cart.

little splashes

▌ Hardware is hot and hip, so give window treatments a trendy look with grommets. Line up a row for hanging or apply them every which way to look like dots.

petal perfect

A simple, classic daisy motif wakes up this basic new-house bathroom.

5 ideas under $100

① Intricate stencils work in a classic bathroom, but for whimsy, simplify the design of a daisy to five petals and a perfectly round, oversize center. Cut two stencils for this pattern: one a flower background to paint white and the other a center circle to layer on top. Or make cardboard templates of the shapes, trace around the templates on the walls using chalk or colored pencils, and fill in with paint. Scatter the flowers across the walls, tucking part of a daisy along the window or bending another around a corner.

② Dress up unfinished wood knobs with polka dots, flowers, or stripes. Use an artist's brush for these small designs. Protect the painted designs with two coats of clear polyurethane.

③ Top a window with a valance made from less than a yard of fabric. Cut two triangles of the same size with one side equal to the window's width plus 1 inch for seam allowance. Place right sides of triangles together, stitch, and turn right side out. Add a plump tassel. Back the valance with a rattan blind that rolls out of sight until bath time. Staple the top of the valance to a 1x2 painted to match the window trim; screw the board to the top of the window frame.

④ Bring in furniture to add utility and character. An old table updated with paint provides a bath-side perch for towels, soaps, and sponges. If a table top is the right size but too tall, shorten the legs. To make a movable table, add casters.

⑤ Make a fun flower rug by starting with a looped bathroom rug. Using a washable fabric pen, draw the outline of the flower on the back of the rug, machine-stitch along this line, cut the rug ½ inch beyond the stitched line, and turn under ½ inch and glue. Fuse the flower rug to a non-slip rug backing.

little splashes

▌ Regularly shop the sale bins at fabric stores. If you spot a beautiful ribbon or trim, buy it when it's greatly discounted, and use it for an instant bathroom pick-me-up. Make ribbon loops to edge a window shade or glue braid to crisscross a lampshade.

just a little splashier

Whimsical style builds on color, and there's plenty of it stocked in stores. The easiest way to create the look is to find a favorite fabric or accessory, and work with those colors.

get the look

▌ Start with easy steps. Ready to try some whimsy in your bathroom? Find an accessory or fabric that pleases you. Place it in the bathroom, and see how it feels after a week or two. If it works, bring in more lighthearted touches.

▌ Practice design restraint. Too many contrasting patterns and colors can seem frantic. Gather potential patterns and colors, and edit down to two or three to include in a small room. Try large patterns as well as small to see how they work.

▌ To experiment with a bold color, paint a test patch of two or three different shades. Observe how sunlight and lamplight affect the colors throughout the day. Consider how the colors blend with wood trim and bathroom fixtures too.

▌ To create a palette of several colors, look to paint manufacturers' color cards to find common tonal values. These colors, located in the same space on the color cards produced by a paint manufacturer, are typically good matches. A no-fail paint scheme mixes two colors in common tones with white.

▌ Keep expensive-to-redo surfaces, such as floors, countertops, and fixtures, in neutral shades. Add color where it's easy and inexpensive to change, such as in wall paint, window coverings, rugs, and accessories.

▌ Search for standard items, such as towels and shower curtains, at discount retailers. Give them whimsical personality with paint and trims, such as fusible flowers and letters.

Paint Be fearless about paint color. It's the cheapest way to freshen up. Try bold colors such as bright green, orange, or yellow. If the color doesn't work for the room, use it to refresh the interior of cabinets.

Fabrics Soften a bathroom and add color punch using bold, fun fabrics. If the project only requires a yard or two, it's easy to fit a budget. For more fabric, check for the pattern using an Internet search engine. For heavy-use bathrooms, consider outdoor fabrics that stand up to humidity and soil.

Paper lanterns Hang lanterns over an old-fashioned clawfoot tub. While soaking away your cares, look up through a canopy of color. Shop import stores for similar lanterns.

Shower curtain Don't be shy about the shower. An adventurous attitude means using a lot of pattern and color. So why not hang a patterned shower curtain? When the curtain looks tired, just replace it with something new. Or buy a top sheet as an inexpensive and stylish option, and back the sheet with a waterproof liner. Be sure to use clip-on shower rings to turn the sheet into an instant and affordable shower curtain.

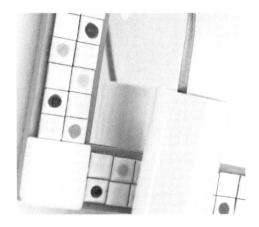

Mirror Paint a mirror to fit the scheme. For this mirror, add 1-inch ceramic tiles around the frame, and accent the tiles using paints suited for glass and ceramics. Check for products and instructions at a crafts store.

Details Remember the details, such as adding a tassel to a window treatment. Finishing touches help a whimsical bathroom come out to play.

Flowers A single bloom instantly brightens any space. Select a variety of vases and rotate the colors to suit the season. If children use the bathroom, look for nonbreakable vases or plastic glasses in fun colors. Check out the inventory at a dollar store for low-cost options.

drawing the lines

Stripes have long been a favorite of designers. They're easy to use and adapt to many looks. Here are two ideas to try.

coloring inside the lines

Paint and painter's tape pair up in this fun project. Although this version started with preprimed canvas, it's easier to use a vinyl remnant. Buy a piece just slightly larger than your finished project, and flip it over to the back side to get started.

HOW TO

paint a floorcloth

1. **Prime** the back side of the vinyl flooring.
2. **Mark** the size of the finished floorcloth using chalk or colored pencils, then mark the center stripes and borders.
3. **Adhere** painter's tape along the chalk marks, pressing tape firmly, *bottom left*.
4. **Dip** a 3-inch roller into any latex paint in a paint tray; blot excess paint on the tray ramp. Roll the paint on the large stripes, *bottom center*; let dry. Repeat the same process using the other paint colors. This project uses light blue, darker blue, and lavender. Carefully remove all tape.
5. **Make** a template for the scalloped edges. Use a paper plate and chalk to trace a half circle onto a scrap of cardboard; cut out.
6. **Trace** the half-circle onto the border using chalk; start in the center of each side of the vinyl remnant. Stop short of the corners and draw the corners freehand to connect adjoining sides. Cut the scalloped border with scissors, *bottom right*.
7. **Seal** the surface with two coats of flat-finish or satin polyurethane; let dry thoroughly between coats. Sand between coats if necessary.

super stripes

These striped accessories, created using colored paper, prove that just a little cash can make a big difference. Use the same technique to cover the mirror mat and to make the framed artwork. It's easy to find colorful papers to fit any color scheme.

▌ To create the mirror frame, remove the mat from the frame, place strips of paper on top of the mat, and wrap the strips around the mat edges. Secure the paper on the back of the mat using double-stick tape. Overlap some of the strips to achieve a 3-D effect. Use the same technique to create the striped artwork on the backsplash.

dressing windows

A little fabric goes a long way in covering bathroom windows. Slim shades and simple curtain panels suit whimsical style while providing privacy.

perfect pears

To create these stylish painted pears, brush various colors of green paint onto a pear stamp, creating highlights and shadows. Test the stamp on a paper scrap to perfect the look. Add more paint to the stamp and stamp the image on the shade at marked points. The pears are 3 inches from the bottom of the shade and 5 inches apart. Reapply paint to the stamp and slightly tilt the stem to vary the angle of each pear. Let dry. Cut gingham ribbon and fusible adhesive material to the width of the shade; follow the manufacturer's instructions to join the fusible adhesive material to the back of the ribbon. Fuse the ribbon to the shade just above the dowel pocket.

purple posies

Fill your bathroom windows with an everblooming garden arranged on a white roller shade. For flower stems, cut ½-inch ribbon in lengths varying from 4 to 24 inches, and hot-glue to the shade, tucking the bottom ½-inch to the back of the shade. Create a simple flower pattern and use it to cut flowers from imitation suede. Cut suede circles that measure 1 inch larger than the grommets needed to attach the flowers. Stack one circle on each flower, place one flower at the top of each stem, and then follow the directions packaged with the grommets to attach the flowers to the shade. Snip the fabric circles to create fringe. For the shade pull, sandwich a flower between two fringed circles, and join using a grommet and grommet tool. Thread ribbon through the grommet, and hand-stitch the ends to the bottom center of the shade. Glue a ribbon bow on top to cover stitching.

modern geometry

Add a personal stamp to a white roller shade for a graphic look that costs less than $12 per shade. Make stamps by gluing craft-foam shapes to pieces of wood; let dry. (This shade design uses three stamps.) Paint the shade a subtle hue or leave it white. Apply paint to portions of the stamp to create a multicolor look. Following a grid marked with chalk, stamp the images in rows across the shade, alternating the pattern with each subsequent row and washing the stamp with water several times during the process to ensure a clean print.

little splashes

■ Before starting a project, practice applying paint to stamps and transferring the image to scrap fabric. Too much paint will result in a sloppy-looking image, while too little won't stamp the shape completely.

jumbo dots

Painted motifs run rings around plain old linen panels. For this oversize dot, trace plates onto the shades to create perfect circles. Use fabric paint and an artist's brush to freehand-paint the shapes onto the curtains. Make sure to follow the paint manufacturer's instructions for preparing, painting, and finishing fabric so the panels can be cleaned.

graphic designs

There's room to play when adopting fresh whimsical style. Here's how with bold shapes and letters.

matchy mats

Double bath-time fun with coordinating mats featuring diamonds. It's no accident that the cutouts are identical.

▌ Cut out large and small paper diamond templates. Center and trace the large diamond and two smaller diamonds on the reverse side of two contrasting-color mats. Using a utility knife and a cutting board, cut out the diamonds on the traced lines; remove. Reposition the diamonds in the contrasting mat. Hand-sew shapes along the raw edges on the wrong sides of the mats using a heavy-duty needle and thread.

wet or dry

Personalize your bath by putting words
on a shower curtain and towels.

▌ Ask a local banner or sign store to make the
shower curtain using the words and colors you
design. Choose white exterior-banner material,
which is water- and mildew-resistant. Or buy a
white cotton shower curtain from a home store
and iron on letters purchased from a crafts store.
For oversize letters, try painting them using fabric
paint. To add words to towels, take them to a
monogramming shop. "Wet" and "dry" make a
playful word combination.

flea market

A bathroom graced with flea market style

revolves around the stuff you love. After all,

designing a bathroom around a collecting

passion is the perfect way to make a bathroom

fun and personal. So line up old flowerpots

on a windowsill, sew shower curtains from vintage

barkcloth, build a vanity from a primitive table, and

relax and bathe in the compliments.

tropical paradise

Old-fashioned fabric prints give this landlocked bathroom a 1940s tropical-beach attitude.

5 ideas under $100

1 In a basic white-tiled bathroom, find the color scheme in the printed hues of a favorite fabric. Pull a soft hue from the fabric design for paint for the walls and a more vibrant tone for towels and accessories; ground the scheme with a neutral, such as white or cream. In many bathrooms the fixtures and tile provide all the neutrals needed.

2 Combine vintage barkcloth patterns that mix but don't match. The tropical palms and repeating coral tones, *opposite*, connect these patterns and stretch skimpy yardage for big projects. Toss in solid-color fabrics with rich texture—even bath towels and loopy bath rugs—to support the old-time prints.

3 Sew a shower curtain from a vintage curtain panel. The slim panel won't cover the tub, but there's enough fabric to hide the plastic liner when it's not in use. To make a wider shower curtain, seam curtain panels together. For a fun effect, alternate curtain patterns to create bold stripes of color and pattern or add solid-color fabrics between fabric-print panels.

4 Use a coordinating fabric for a sink skirt. To make it work, stitch a narrow casing along the top edge, slip elastic through the casing, and secure it to the wall on both sides. Stretch the elastic around the edge of the vanity to hold the skirt in place. To create lots of gathers, sew a skirt that's double the width of the area to be covered. For storage under the sink, purchase a tall wicker basket that fits under the drain pipes or several smaller baskets to nestle side by side. Line them all with more of the barkcloth.

5 Bring out flea market collections to use as accessories and to add a touch of nostalgia. Pottery in shades of green adds color. Use it for plants on the windowsill, or repurpose the pots to corral bathroom supplies on the vanity. Perch old oil paint-by-number artwork on the windowsill for a bit of mid-century kitsch. For a cohesive look and a blast from the past, collect by era or color.

little splashes

▌ Before buying, check flea market furniture for warped wood that's caused by exposure to moisture. Cabinet doors are highly susceptible. It takes an experienced woodworker—and money—to repair this type of damage.

bathing beauty

Floral prints and a snappy red floor make this small bathroom a happy retreat.

5 ideas under $100

1. In bathrooms with dated wall tiles, the first change has to be the walls. Depending on the size of the bathroom, it's possible to cover the walls with cement-board exterior siding.

2. Once painted, it's impervious to all the water a bathroom dishes out. Ask a skilled friend to help with this project.

   Stop the siding short of the ceiling, and top it with crown molding that serves as a shallow display shelf. Paint the foot of space between the molding and the ceiling sky blue, a hue that offers a fresh look overhead. If the walls just need paint, consider stopping the wall color short of the ceiling and duplicating the effect of molding using paint.

3. A bright floor punches up a small space. The commercial vinyl tiles in sizzling red complement the vintage style of the room. If spreading the commercial tile adhesive seems too messy, look for tile squares with peel-and-stick backs. Make sure the floor is clean and smooth before applying either type of tile.

4. Flowery fabric softens a room filled with slick surfaces. Floral sheets in a vintage pattern stand in as a shower curtain; double panels pulled back on each side of the tub give the effect of a window treatment. For the window, a vintage curtain panel acts as a Roman shade. To make the shade, nail the corners of the panel to the window trim; hide the nailheads with glued-on buttons. Cut and stitch narrow lengths of fabric to tie around the panels and hold them in place. The vanity, made by installing a sink in an old table, includes an attached skirt that conceals the sink's plumbing and storage.

5. Bring in collections to add character. A well-used kitchen stool holds an assortment of favorite finds. The deep window ledge provides room for a framed botanical print and pretty glassware. To widen a narrow window ledge, add a shelf that's level with the sill. Enhance the theme with a flowered platter hung on the wall. It's the perfect moisture-proof art.

little splashes

For a vintage look in the bathroom, search Web sites for stylish reproductions. Select from fixtures, fabrics, flooring, and accessories with an olden glow.

just a little splashier

It's time to go shopping. The best way to build a flea market bathroom is to find vintage or reproduction items. Look for printed fabrics, collectible dishes, and kitschy oil paintings as a foundation for style.

get the look

▮ Folks who love the flea market look are already collectors, so it's easy to start the bathroom makeover by matching a color palette to collected items. The trick is to select a range of colors—neutrals and pastels—that recede so the collections take the spotlight.

▮ Shop for functional vintage furniture that fits the bathroom. Consider tables or dressers for use as vanities. Measure shelves and cupboards to hang on the walls for storage. Gather baskets and chairs for use as tub-side tables.

▮ Look for reproduction fixtures and fittings that suit the collections. Try searching on the Internet by typing in "reproduction bathroom fixtures." Or shop a salvage yard for oldies but goodies.

▮ Repurpose vintage finds to create storage with style. Stash extra towels in vintage hatboxes, gather jewelry on wood-burned trays, and fill a covered wicker basket with soaps.

▮ Mass collections to create a focal point. If one vintage printed fabric is good, two are even better. A single milk-glass plate looks lonely on the wall; a collection of plates makes a statement. Pair up any collection to create a dramatic look that's perfectly personal and unexpected.

▮ Buy extras to swap out when you want a change in the bathroom. When it's hard to decide which flea-market look is best, buy both. Just make sure the backgrounds—walls, floors, and fixtures—can support either look.

Wallpaper Purchase a roll of wallpaper at a big discount by shopping the "returns" room at a wallpaper store. Use the paper to line shelves or drawers in the bathroom; they will make any room feel special.

Frames Shop for frames with or without art, and resell any art that isn't needed. Frames that require painting or fixing are often the best bargains. If the frame is damaged, cut away the bad parts and make a smaller, flawless frame.

Kitchen glass Utilitarian glass pieces meant for the kitchen look great filled with bath salts. If the holes in the shaker top are too small for bath salts, enlarge them using an awl. File down rough spots on the inside of the top.

Colorful tablecloths Forget about the table. Think of these fun squares of pattern as the raw material for sink skirts, shower curtains, and window coverings. If the tablecloths are stained, don't worry. Just cut around the bad parts.

Washbasin A floral-painted enamelware basin makes a fun sink. Buy a basin big enough for splashing and install the faucet in the countertop.

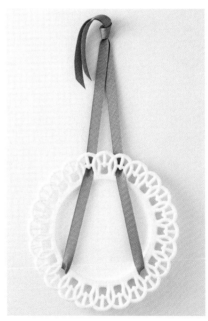

Plate art Hang a single plate or a wall of plates. It's cheap and easy when you start with affordable milk-glass plates with cutwork borders. Simply slip ribbon through the openings to create a plate hanger.

Flowerpots McCoy introduced colorful flowerpots—green, pink, yellow, and cream—in the late 1920s and '30s. A favorite of collectors, these pots and their look-alike cousins can be used to add flair and function to a flea market bathroom.

more for less

Instead of just collecting, collect with a purpose: to turn lovable finds into useful items for the bathroom. Think window treatments, storage containers, towel bars, and vintage dressers.

striped by hand

Stripes on the wall provide a graphic backdrop for all things collected from the flea market. The process is easy enough for a patient beginner and a snap for an experienced painter.

HOW TO

stripe a wall with paint

1. **Tape off** moldings, trim, and ceiling using quick-release painter's tape that won't leave any sticky residue. Paint walls using an off-white base coat of latex paint; let dry.
2. **Plan** stripes to fit the scale of the room; a width of 3 to 6 inches works best in a small space. Using a measuring tape and a colored pencil, mark off 6-inch-wide stripes spaced 4 inches apart. To avoid folding a stripe around a corner, fudge the measurements a bit.
3. **Use** a level and a colored pencil to extend the marks from just under the ceiling line to the floor, *below left*. The level serves as a straightedge for the penciled lines. The stripes are measured and marked, but not taped off.
4. **Paint** stripes freehand on the wall in 12-inch sections using a 2- or 3-inch-wide paintbrush, *below right*. Start at the top and paint down each side, drawing the edge of the paintbrush along the penciled lines. Fill in the stripes before the paint dries along the edges. The look will be soft and painterly rather than crisp.

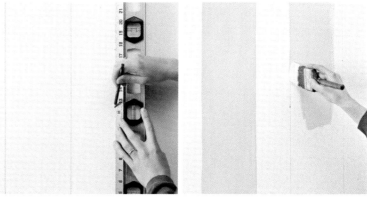

top it off

Start with a vintage tablecloth to make this easy, no-sew window treatment, *right* and *above*. Fold the tablecloth diagonally and secure it to the window frame with drapery tacks. Look for fun tacks with decorative ends, such as the starfish, *above*. The treatment is flexible enough to use almost any size tablecloth for any size window: the ends drape on the sides. If there's a rip or stain in the tablecloth, just turn it to the window side.

hang it up

Look for the ingredients for these funky towel racks, *above*, at a home center. Make one towel rack from nippled plumbing pipe cut to the desired length, two 90-degree elbows, two 1-inch pieces of nippled pipe, and two flanges, *above right*. Assemble the towel bar by screwing the short nippled pipe into the flanges and then into the elbows. Add the long nippled pipe last. For rust protection, spray the pipe with automotive paint before installing the bar. Attach the towel bar to the wall, securing screws through the openings in the flanges. Use wall anchors to screw the towel bars into drywall.

wall art

A sliver of wall is all the space needed to create a dramatic display of found objects.

mirror magic

Mirrors offer magical space-expanding capabilities. For a dramatic effect, group a collection of mirrors to reflect the room. Frameless mirrors work best because they appear to float on the wall.

Attach hangers to the plywood mirror backs, selecting hangers suitable for the weight of the mirrors. Hanging several mirrors ensures that there's one at the perfect height for everyone in the family.

not just for dinner

Turn a spare corner of the bathroom into a showcase for collections, *right*. It's all about the composition. Build it up the wall with a grouping of creamy plates hung in a grid. If the bathroom is small, this might fill the space. If there's more room, snuggle an old table underneath the plates, and top it with an embroidered tablecloth placed on the diagonal. Gather an assortment of favorite things to use for bathroom supplies—a lidded compote for cotton balls, old bottles for lotions, and a pressed-glass bowl for jewelry.

storage bonus

Bathroom supplies take up space. Give them a place that's practical and stylish with a simple white shelf lined with hooks, *below*. Painting the shelf white and using white towels and accessories keeps the look clean and uncluttered, perfect for what is often the smallest room in the house.

spa

Spas and relaxation go together like symphonies and classical music. Orchestrate a revitalizing concerto at home with simple luxuries, soft colors, aromatic scents, and relaxing ingredients that ensure a refuge that leaves stress at the door. Think of the style of a spa bathroom as the at-home equivalent of a serene and expensive spa. Ready to unwind and slow down? Here's how to get started.

day spa

Natural woods, cool stone, and soft colors give this treetop bathroom the peaceful feeling of a Zen retreat.

5 ideas under $100

1. Opt for light woods and simple cabinetry. If the vanity is already dark, paint it a lighter shade that mimics a wood tone. To give it the look of wood, use a graining tool (roller grainer or heart grainer) and a tinted glaze to create a new finish that looks like natural wood. Protect the faux-grained finish with a coat or two of polyurethane. For wood-graining tools, check out home improvement stores, paint stores, or type "faux wood grain" into an online search engine. Choose simple hardware for a clean, minimalist look.

2. Furniture and accessories with an Oriental attitude contribute to the spa look. Select from rustic chairs, a stool, and simple wood stands to hold stacks of white towels. Wrap soap bars in textured rice paper to pair beauty with aroma. Purchase woven slippers for an after-bath treat.

3. Bring in relaxing textures with a shag rug to soften tile floors, slubby linen for shades, rough wood for accessories, and smooth wood for cabinetry. To add even more texture, consider a wall covering that looks like bamboo sticks or grasscloth. Use the wall covering to wrap around the room like a wainscot or to cover storage boxes. A bamboo floor mat can also offer spa texture underfoot.

4. Add a touch of nature with fresh-picked flowers anchored in smooth rocks. For an arrangement that lasts, purchase a few tropical leaves instead of blooms. Select flowers or leaves with interesting branches to show through a clear glass container. Select a large container if you have the counter space.

5. Spare window treatments invite the outdoors in. Blinds that pull up tight to the window frame provide a view while the sun shines and offer privacy at night. Consider blinds of coarse woven fabric, rice paper, or natural bamboo.

little splashes

For a one-of-a-kind floor, purchase 12-inch-square vinyl tiles in an assortment of similar colors and cut them into 3-inch stripes or 6-inch squares. Install in a variegated pattern.

bathing retreat

This vintage clawfoot tub is used for soaking only. It's the ideal way to relax and get away without ever leaving home.

5 ideas under $100

1 Start with a restful color scheme of sage, cream, khaki, and soft white to create the backdrop for a room meant for relaxing. To keep the space bright, wrap white wainscoting around the bottom of the room and repeat the color on the trim. For a coordinated tint, add a small amount of the sage green paint to the white; try just a few drops per quart. Keep adding small amounts of paint until you have the color you want.

2 Turn a clawfoot tub into the focal point of a home spa. After all, a warm bath is an ancient remedy for rejuvenating yourself after a stressful day. A clawfoot tub might seem more cottagey than Zen-like, but choose the look that's most relaxing and personal.

3 Keep spa paraphernalia close at hand. Suspend a bath rack across the tub to hold pretty potions and aromatic soaps. If there's more room, snuggle a small table or stool near the tub to hold even more scented products. Make space for towels by installing a decorative curtain rod under the windowsill. Add a center support to keep the rod from sagging.

4 If privacy isn't an issue, leave windows uncovered to let in light and views of the sky. If you need to block views from neighbors, keep the look clean and spare with Roman shades that pull up out of the way or blinds that roll from the bottom up. Or consider decorative window films that screen the view and add style. Look for options including films that look like lace, stained glass, frosted glass, glass pebbles, mirror tiles, and more.

5 Gather items with a rustic or outdoorsy touch to add character to the space. Use a woven wicker basket as a wastepaper basket. Hang a shelf with peeling paint as a focal point. Showcase well-used pottery pieces on a windowsill, or keep the pottery filled with blooming plants or aromatic herbs. Add a vintage wicker rocking chair that withstands moisture and offers a relaxing rocking motion to soothe away the cares of the day. Cushion the seat and add a few pillows for extra comfort.

little splashes

Music, aromatic candles, and scented lotions can turn any bathroom into a temporary spa. Gather the ingredients in a basket that's easy to pull out when there's time to soak in the tub. Purchase oversize bath sheets or terry-cloth robes for after-bath lounging.

just a little splashier

Gather objects made for pampering, and they'll create a bathroom that's long on relaxation and full of good scents.

get the look

▌ A spa bathroom should feel peaceful and serene. Start the makeover by creating a background of relaxing colors—taupes, soft blues and greens, and restful tans. Look for fabrics, paint, and accessories in a narrow range of tones.

▌ Incorporate natural woods and materials in the scheme. That might mean lightly-stained wood for cabinetry and woodwork, stone-look countertops, and bamboo flooring.

▌ Add interest with texture. Consider terry cloth, burlap, and linen for fabrics; teak, maple, and cherry for woods; rattan for baskets and blinds; and just-picked branches to celebrate the season. Incorporate accessories, such as handmade bowls and soaps.

▌ Search for furniture that adds beauty and function. For calm, add pieces such as cabinets that hide clutter. If there's room, include a chair or small table that's easy to pull up to the tub to hold soaps and towels. Wheels on the table or chair make it easy to move.

▌ Lighting in the spa bathroom has to be bright for grooming, yet soft and relaxing for soaking in the tub. Ask an experienced friend to install a dimmer on all bathroom lights. If that isn't possible, add a candle chandelier over the tub, or a shelf by the tub that's filled with votives.

▌ Favorite aromas add the final luxury. Search for natural scents in soaps, candles, and lotions. Vary the selection to suit the season.

Scented soaps Bars of lavender and patchouli soap add aroma to the bathroom even when they're just filling a bowl. To keep your favorite scents in stock, buy extra bars, wrap them in rice paper, and heap them to overflowing in a handmade bowl.

Herbal bouquets Turn the tub into an herbal sauna by tying sprigs of sage, lavender, thyme, French tarragon, and mint to the faucet. Let hot water splash over the herb bouquet to create a fragrant steam bath.

Fluffy towels A restful bathroom doesn't have to be monochromatic. Add subtle color with soft, textured towels and bath sheets to use as window treatments and shower curtains. Purchase woven trims to decorate the bottom edges.

Rattan baskets Clutter has no place in a restful spa, so keep all the bits and pieces of bathroom supplies stowed away in matching rattan baskets. Slip the baskets inside a cabinet or make room for them on an open shelf.

Tub-side chair A chair does double duty in a spa bathroom. Use it to keep stacks of absorbent towels at hand during bathing or to provide a convenient perch for dressing. It's easy to move the chair wherever it's needed.

Showerheads Rain offers a soft tempo and relaxing sound. Create a similar effect with an oversize showerhead that delivers water in a fine spray. Before buying, consider the size of the shower enclosure and the spray pattern of the showerhead.

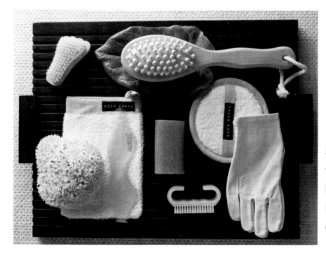

Spa gear Find a beautiful wood tray and fill it with pampering things: a natural sea sponge; brushes for feet, back massage, and nails; loofah soap; a linen bath mitt; and an herbal eye compress.

make it yours

The time spent creating projects for a spa reaps big returns in comfort and relaxation. Think first about what matters most, then set to work.

paint a little texture

A floorcloth offers added warmth and texture for the bathroom floor. The easy paint method guarantees perfect results.

HOW TO

paint a floorcloth

1. **Make** a floorcloth using a vinyl flooring remnant and a notched squeegee. To notch the squeegee, use a crafts knife to cut evenly spaced teeth along its rubber edge.
2. **Prime** the back side of the vinyl, and apply a coat of floor paint. Try one of the new floor paints that offer almost endless color choices and better durability.
3. **Let** the paint dry. Tape off a grid of 1-foot squares using a checkerboard pattern. Plan the color and pattern of each square, and indicate them on a piece of painter's tape stuck to each square. Remove the tape from the squares before painting.
4. **Brush** contrasting paint in the taped-off squares; pull the squeegee through the paint before it dries. Remove tape; let the paint dry.
5. **Re-tape** the remaining squares to finish painting. Brush contrasting paint in the taped-off squares, pulling a squeegee perpendicular to the dry squares. Use a zigzag motion with the squeegee to make a herringbone pattern. Remove tape; let the paint dry.
6. **Seal** the entire floorcloth with at least two coats of polyurethane.

easy-sew coverup

For washable comfort and a cool spa look, create a terry-cloth pinafore for a classic wood folding chair.

HOW TO
dress a spa chair

1. **Sand**, prime, and paint the chair using semigloss latex paint.
2. **Cut** two pieces of terry cloth, each as wide as the chair, plus 1 inch for seam allowances. For the length, measure from the front of the chair seat to the back, up the back, and back down to the seat; add 18 inches (two 9-inch drops) and 1 inch for seam allowances.
3. **With** right sides facing, sew the two strips together on all edges using ½-inch seams. Leave an opening for turning; turn the cover to the right side and slipstitch closed.
4. **Place** the cover on the chair. Cut four 18-inch lengths of grosgrain ribbon. Tack pairs of ribbons on either side of the cover where the seat joins the back. Tie ribbons to hold the cover in place.

scented face scrub

For a revitalizing homemade face scrub, follow these steps.

HOW TO
make a scented scrub

1. **Finely** grate 1 cup of natural soap, such as castile; set aside.
2. **Chop** dried peel of one orange; set aside.
3. **Mix** 2 cups whole oats, 1 cup nonfat powdered milk, and 1 cup dried rose petals in large bowl.
4. **Add** grated soap and chopped orange peel to bowl and stir.
5. **Blend** all ingredients into a powder using a food processor; pour into an airtight container.
6. **Place** ⅓ cup of the blended powder in the center of a washcloth. Tie into a pouch, dampen, and use to exfoliate your face. Hang the pouch to dry. Replace after several uses.

spa storage

Bathroom gear, including towels and bottles, may be stylish enough to put on display. Try these ideas.

shelf it up

The ingredients of a spa—fluffy white towels, glass bottles filled with scented liquids, and pails of soaps—easily set the getaway mood. Give each item its own space in a vintage cabinet painted chocolate brown. Whether the cabinet stands open all the time or only occasionally, the order and beauty inside is sure to lower stress levels. To paint an old cabinet, lightly sand the finish, fill holes, apply a coat of primer, and then finish with two coats of semigloss brown paint. To decorate the cabinet windows, use sheets of frosted paper or window film. Shop a local crafts store for pretty papers to tape in place or a home center for window film.

two for show

Pair a lone dining room chair with a vintage hospital table for an eclectic look that works in the spa bathroom. The rolling table can slip over one end of the tub, and the chair doubles as towel storage. Look for items like these at flea markets or garage sales. For a more modern look, shop for a new plastic stool to take the hospital table's place next to the sudsy water and a water-resistant chair to sit by its side.

nest away

A spa bathroom is bound to be popular with guests. Make them feel welcome by filling a woven carrier with lotions, candles, room fragrances, bath oils, and soaps. Keep a collection of pretty glass bottles to hold the scented powders and oils. Place the carrier on a tray with a stack of white towels, stash the tray and its contents in a closet between guest visits, or make a spa tray for your own daily use.

little splashes

▌ Order adhesive words or sayings to apply to bathroom walls. Search online by typing "adhesive letters" into a search engine. Pick the words that suit the style of the decor.

stack and hang

There's nothing restful about piles of dirty towels on the bathroom floor. Keep the space in order with a pretty peg rack screwed to the wall. It provides plenty of room for towels to dry. For a large family, add a letter above each peg so each person has their own spot. Make a quick towel rack by installing a row of hooks on the molding below the windowsill.

beac

It's not surprising that the beach inspires a favorite bathroom style. After all, water plays the pivotal role in both locations. So pour it on with style that makes the most of the soft tones of sand and surf, and wraps it up with accessories that make a beach vacation a daily memory.

Listen closely. Isn't the beach calling?

by the beach

Give any bathroom a vacation attitude with a wash of light colors and shell-adorned accessories inspired by the beach.

5 ideas under $100

1 Bring in the color of sky and water using glass mosaic tiles. Let the rest of the space recede with a soft coat of white paint. Glass mosaic tiles come glued on 12×12-inch vinyl backing for easy installation. Mosaic tiles can be used on floors and walls. Check out page 98 for a mirror project finished with glass mosaic tiles.

2 Collect flea market furniture and use it for storage, whether it's for long term or the length of a soak in the tub. Look for multipurpose wood pieces that can be painted in soft blues, greens, and whites to fit the beachy look. Move the pieces where you need them, such as next to the tub or under a window to hold bath supplies.

3 Personal touches, such as towels monogrammed in a curvy font, make a bathroom special. For a beach attitude, pair sandy beige with watery blue. Check for local embroidery businesses that offer a broad selection of font types and thread colors. Most provide a preview of the final look and size on a computer screen before stitching begins. Consider adding a monogram to a chair slipcover or a shower curtain as well.

4 A chandelier layered with shells makes a bold statement. A shell-encrusted chandelier can cost upwards of $800, but you can make one at home using collected or purchased shells and a ratty chandelier found at a flea market. The trick is to find the right adhesive for gluing shells to a metal surface. Most epoxy glues or construction adhesives will work, but always test a product in a small area. Cover surfaces with one variety of small shells; use large shells to add drama.

5 Finish a beach bathroom with tropical accents, including bamboo blinds and a mirror edged with faux bamboo. The rich tones of the bamboo keep the look from seeming too soft. Gather shells to fill bowls and baskets, to rest on a window frame, or to serve as a doorstop. To make a large shell into a doorstop, fill it with plaster of paris to increase its weight.

little splashes

▌Make art for your bathroom by framing favorite quotes—printed in color—and hanging them one above the other on a slice of wall.

looking up

Texture rather than color gives this tall but small bathroom its style oomph.

5 ideas under $100

① If there's only room for a little bit of tile, place it on the focal point wall, the one that's visible from the bathroom door. Look for affordable tiles at the home center or flooring store. If the bathroom is already tiled but the color is dated, consider painting the tile white for a fresh look. Start the process with a primer made for use on tile. That's a good solution for areas outside a shower enclosure. Camouflage the shower tile behind a shower curtain.

② Think vertically in a small space. That's one way to draw attention away from small square footage. Vertical lines are created by a pedestal sink and tall mirror that stretches the view. To take advantage of vertical space, hang the shower curtain from the ceiling instead of from the top of the tub surround, or drape a window treatment from the top of the wall instead of from just above the window molding.

③ Create one elegant showstopper—a shell-encrusted mirror—to give a bathroom a big dose of beach style. To make this mirror, start with a wood mirror that's worn and old, or cut the shape for a mirror from a sheet of ½-inch plywood. Paint the plywood to match the shell color, and glue mirror cut to size to the plywood. Glue shells to the wood frames using adhesive suitable for both materials.

④ New classic sconces that match the faucet freshen the lighting. To update existing sconces, mask off the surrounding area and treat the sconces to a fresh coat of metallic spray paint. For an aged metal look, consider a paint that includes flakes of real metal that will tarnish with exposure to humidity.

⑤ Add textural details, such as a woven wicker basket for trash and a wire stand for bath gear. Hooks mounted on the bathroom door offer a temporary spot for a bathrobe or beach bag.

little splashes

Incorporate the season's hottest colors by buying 2-ounce bottles of paint to add just a touch of fresh color to accessories.

just a little splashier

Collect the raw ingredients for this bathroom makeover during walks on the beach. Bring them home, whether your bath is near water or surrounded by land.

get the look

▌ The palette for a beachy bathroom is easy. Simply pull paint colors that match sand, surf, and sky. Use the soft tones as a background for splashes of bright accent colors. The neutral hues make it easy to layer on almost any color, and to change colors on a whim.

▌ Look to the beach for materials to create the room's focal point. The material might be glass mosaic tile that looks like beach glass, or shells that can be incorporated into a mirror surround or light fixture. These elements anchor the look.

▌ Minimize patterns and play up textures. Look for ways to combine rough and smooth. Try pairing shiny ceramic tile with rattan blinds, or a rustic wood stool with glass mosaic tile.

▌ Add the shimmer of sunlight reflecting on water by hanging mirrors on more than one wall. Opting for shiny versus matte tiles and using glass containers and vases can spread the glimmer from one end of the bathroom to the other.

▌ Create storage that reflects the beach. It might be as simple as hanging a row of beach totes from hooks along one wall, or letting rolling waves inspire the design of a shelf.

▌ Beach-friendly accessories offer water-resistant touches. Bring shell-encrusted mirrors or boxes home from a beach vacation and add photographs of the family frolicking in the surf. Stretch bamboo beach mats on the floor in place of bathroom rugs.

Glass tile Bring home the look of beach glass with mosaic tiles in a rainbow of colors. Look for mosaic pieces in squares and rectangles, and in vitreous and iridescent glass.

Shell accessories The Victorians loved to add shells to everything from trinket boxes to frames. Look for shell-covered frames to buy or add your own shells to purchased frames. Make sure to use an epoxy glue to keep the shells sticking tight in a humid bathroom.

Glass canister Keep favorite shells in a lidded glass canister to enjoy their sand-rubbed colors without fear of dust.

Glass bottles Gather a collection of new glass that repeats the colors of beach glass. Vary the shapes so the vases look appealing with and without flowers. Group them on a sunny shelf or windowsill so the sun shines through. For a similar effect, purchase clear glass vases and fill them with beach glass. Look for assorted colors of beach glass that's sold by the pound and half pound.

Shell candelabra A little excess can be a good thing—just imagine pairing candlelight and shells. Find an elegantly shaped candelabra at a flea market, test the arms for strength (shells can add a lot of weight), then start gluing shells to the surfaces. Create texture with small shells on the curving arms and large shells on the base.

Wire baskets These handy carryalls stand in as shell-collecting vessels on the beach. At home, fill them with towels, sponges, or lotions. They simplify carting gear from storage cabinets to the tub.

Shelf A ledge at the head of the tub provides just enough space for holding soaps and lotions. Secure a single board to brackets painted white. It recalls a Nantucket beach cottage, particularly when paired with beaded-board paneling.

from the sea

Look for inspiration for a beach bathroom in everything from the rolling curls of waves to the soft colors of sea and sand.

catch a wave

A repeating wave pattern graces this small shelf. Make one to fit a bathroom wall.

HOW TO

make this scalloped shelf

1. **Measure** the shelf size and create a scallop pattern by dividing the length into equal half-circles. Mark the size of the scallops on kraft paper, then use the edge of a plate to create a gentle curve for each scallop. Make a pattern for the side pieces too.
2. **Transfer** the patterns to a 1×6 or 1×8 board cut to the length needed.
3. **Using** a saber saw, cut one front and two sides using the scallop patterns. Cut the top to the length needed.
4. **Assemble** the pieces using wood glue and screws, attaching the top to the front, *below left,* and a side on each end, *below right.*
5. **Sand** the surface lightly, remove dust with a tack cloth, and prime the wood surface, sanding between paint coats. Apply at least two coats of semigloss paint.

frosty flowers

No matter where they're set, these etched-look vases recall memories of beach glass. To make them, use self-adhesive labels or shaped stickers to create a simple pattern. Using glass frost spray paint, spray the exterior of the vase until it's frosty all over. Let the paint dry and peel off the stickers to reveal the crystal-clear shapes beneath.

little splashes

Pair a table runner with clip-on curtain hardware to create an instant valance. For other options, consider place mats, pillowcases, and hand towels.

details

A simple bowl of shells or a swag of sand dollars reflects the beach.

full to the brim

Sometimes the easiest project can be a simple favorite. That's the case with this bowl of shells. Gather a white bowl and pile it full of shells. For variety, combine a selection of shells and coral. If a beach vacation is months away, search for shells online or at a flea market. Set a big bowl of shells on a bathside table, or place a small bowl near the sink.

shell swag

Turn a beach walk into a reminder of a favorite vacation by assembling a window swag from beach finds. To make the swag, collect shells and sand dollars and purchase small beads. Use the natural holes in the sand dollars for ribbon hangers; glue jewelry caps to the ends of shells to hang. String the beads on heavy thread to make the swags. Hang the shells and sand dollars on the swags.

star finish

Top a bathroom window with blue glass bottles to evoke the color of water. Stand elegant starfish between the bottles. To create a dramatic perch for a collection, install crown molding on top of the window molding to duplicate the look of a triangular pediment. Use a miter saw to cut the angles on the molding; attach it to the wall using construction adhesive and nails. Fill any gaps with caulk. Prime and then paint the pediment the same color as the room's millwork. If the top of the window is too narrow to serve as a shelf, add a piece of wood to the windowsill.

say cheese

Remember the fun with black-and-white photography inspired by the bath and the beach. To use sentimental or valuable photographs in a moisture-filled bathroom, color-copy them and store the originals. Frame the photocopies to create a wainscot above the tub. The frames are different sizes but made from molding of the same thickness and color. Draw a level line with a pencil and a carpenter's level. Screw through the frames' edges to keep the framed photos level.

all for vanity

Whether built from a brand-new cabinet or created from a vintage piece, the vanity is the heart of the bathroom.

off-the-shelf makeover

A stock vanity base and plywood cut into a mirror shape offer affordable style that's easy to customize. Start with beach basics including shells and 1-inch-square glass tiles.

HOW TO

create the vanity and mirror

1. **Mark** an x from corner to corner on the flat panels of the cabinet doors.
2. **Cut** one strip of wood to fit diagonally across the panels. Mark where it meets the routed edges and cut at an angle with a coping saw.
3. **Repeat** for the opposite side, but cut the strip into two pieces to cross the first strip. Glue in place. Caulk gaps and paint.
4. **Cut** the mosaic mirror shape from ½-inch plywood using a saber saw. Screw to the wall around an existing mirror.
5. **Remove** the 1-inch-square glass tiles from the paper backing by soaking them in water. This lets the tiles butt together and eliminates the need for grout. Glue the tiles to the plywood mirror frame using clear acrylic adhesive caulk. Stop the tiles short of the top to allow space for the crown of shells.
6. **Secure** shells to the top of the pediment, using a large featured shell in the center. To secure heavier shells, apply epoxy or thick white crafts glue to them and support them with small nails. Glue lighter and smaller shells along the top curved edge until the pediment is covered.

winning pairs

The grayed tones of aged paint and natural shells make comfortable decorating partners. To create these companion pieces, top a vintage gray-painted dresser with a mirror surrounded by layers of sand dollars. Use wood glue to adhere the sand dollars to the mirror frame and to each other. Glue the sand dollars to the frame's base. Glue a second layer of smaller sand dollars over the first. Let dry completely before hanging. Use special shells as bottle stoppers for a dresser-top display.

cour

There's no doubting the universal appeal of country style,

a look that's loved as much for its ties to the past

as for the subtle updates that keep it fresh for today.

Look for country's updated attitude in bathrooms

that showcase the best of the style

with simpler shapes, bolder stencil and

fabric patterns, fresher colors, and less clutter.

Here's how to make old new again.

try

new age

A new house might seem an unlikely location for a vintage country look, but here's proof that age is a matter of perception.

5 ideas under $100

① Panel a wall with wood planks nailed horizontally. On a tight budget limit the project to one wall. To make it look aged, paint the pine boards with watered-down waterbase paint. The wood knots will slowly begin to show through the paint as the oil in the wood bleeds through the finish.

② For a more rustic look, buy salvage boards to install on the walls, and seal them with a coat of polyurethane to withstand bathroom moisture.

The vanity is often the showpiece of a bathroom, so make it country by creating one from a scrubbed pine table. Look for a table that's wide enough to hold a sink basin and a countertop-mounted faucet. Protect the table's surface with two coats of matte polyurethane. To minimize the appearance of pipes under the sink, use a few baskets on the shelf as a partial cover-up. To hide the plumbing completely, hang a skirt from the table's apron.

③ Buy an old claw-foot tub for less than $100 by shopping salvage yards, flea markets, and yard sales. It's best to buy local or the cost of shipping will eat up the budget. Look for a tub with a good finish so it can be installed "as is."

④ Country storage is meant to be seen and noticed, so fill open baskets with towels, stack lotions and potions on shelves, and stow rolls of toilet paper in wood crates. It's a great way to get organized, an easy place to store products where they're used, and a quick reminder when supplies are running low. For hidden storage, make room for an old dresser or pie safe. The doors and drawers keep things handy without cluttering the space. To update a vintage piece with an authentic finish, try milk paint, which is made from the same basic ingredients used 100 years ago.

⑤ Accessories add personality and vintage flavor to a bathroom. Consider hooked or braided rugs for the floor, maple sugar buckets for vases, vintage trays to hold grooming supplies, and old porcelain switch and outlet covers instead of new plastic ones. For vintage-look lighting fixtures, check at home centers and search online by typing "reproduction lighting" in a search engine. When buying new accessories, look for items with classic country shapes and muted colors that blend with vintage items.

little splashes

Even a line of paint at wainscot height freshens a bathroom. An artist's brush and a carpenter's level create a painterly line; use painter's tape to add a crisp stripe.

bathroom reform

A bathroom under the eaves proves that it's smart to enhance a room's architectural style with paint and accessories.

5 ideas under $100

1. Whether bathroom walls are sloped or straight, tongue-and-groove beaded-board wainscoting on the lower wall adds texture. Get the look for less by using 4×8-foot sheets of pine plywood that's grooved to look like beaded-board and has tongue-and-groove edges.

2. A subtle color palette firmly grounds a bathroom with country style. Soft greens and blues look fresh paired with crisp white woodwork. A room with a lot of angles can look too busy if the colors strongly contrast. Look for other soft hues by selecting from the lightest colors on a paint card. Save bold colors to use as accents, such as red in the rug and green for accessories. A subtle color palette also makes it easy to change accent colors to suit the season.

3. When it comes to country style, collections give any space a finished look. Create country-cool accessories by framing a vintage print in a rustic frame, filling a covered dish with bath salts, and stacking a watering can nearby. Old French toweling stretched alongside a tub serves as a long and slim rug. A touch of greenery brings out the room's color scheme.

4. Turn floor baskets into laundry storage: one for dirty towels and one for clean. Stashed in a corner, they're handy and add fun texture.

5. Old stuff creates the right country attitude, but don't look for pieces with pedigrees. A ragtag dresser that's missing its mirror can add just the right vintage note at an affordable price. If it's not the perfect color, feel free to paint it. Lightly sand the finish, apply a coat of primer, and brush on two coats of latex paint. For a worn look, use steel wool or sandpaper to distress the edges. Line the drawers with vintage fabrics or pretty papers, and toss in the stuff you want to keep under cover.

little splashes

For an extra-tall shower curtain, buy terry cloth by the yard and cut to length. Use clip-on curtain rings to hang it in place.

just a little splashier

Comfort rules in a country bathroom, so look for towels and linens with touch-me texture and soft colors subdued with gray.

get the look

▮ The easiest way to select a country paint palette is to go shopping with a fabric or accessory. The grayed shades that work best with country collections are easy to find using a color sample. Start your search with the historic lines most paint companies carry.

▮ Look for pieces in natural wood; they will blend with the antiques used in the space. Incorporate wood floors, cabinetry, or accessories to lend a touch of age.

▮ Search online for knobs, window hardware, faucets, and towel bars that look old even though they're brand new.

▮ Create spaces for hiding clutter. Today's fresh country look is sparer and lighter than it was 30 years ago. The good news is that many collectibles—rattan baskets, wood carryalls, painted cabinets, and metal buckets—serve as roomy storage containers.

▮ Lighten up by covering windows just enough for privacy. A simple curtain panel, spare Roman shade, roller shade, or clean-lined blind pairs privacy with style.

▮ Nicks and scratches add to this family-friendly style. Look for vintage pieces, such as scrubbed-top tables, that look even better as they age.

Wood stool A folding camp stool makes a stylish landing pad for towels. Fold the towels casually, or roll them up in a basket. For a soft look, pair white towels with a natural wood stool. For a surprise, combine colorful towels with a painted stool.

Braided rugs Once handmade by pioneer women, braided rugs were crafted from fabric strips cut from old blankets and clothing. Look for new versions in fresh colors and folk art patterns.

Shelf A pair of brackets can turn any board into a useful shelf. Stack three or four shelves up the wall to take the place of a linen closet.

Paint Use paint to create style for less. Try these pastel shades to update furniture, change a wall, or frame a mirror.

Hardware Hooks in various sizes and shapes offer decorating flexibility and hand-wrought appeal. Use them for hanging curtains, towels, and baskets with handles. Some hooks have points that hammer into the wall; others screw in place or hang from a rod.

Faux finish To age the finish on new cabinetry, try this technique. Brush stain on the cabinets, then wipe and blot it off with a rag. Let the stain dry for a day, and repeat the process until the finish looks aged. Seal the surface with two coats of polyurethane, lightly sanding between coats.

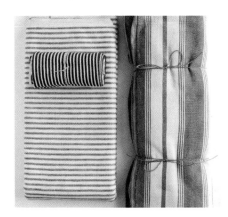

Ticking New or old, ticking is practical and hardworking. Use it for shower curtains, window treatments, and sink skirts. Feel free to mix and match stripes of various sizes but opt for shades of one color.

Bench A narrow bench is the most adaptable of accessories. Its lean lines fit almost anywhere, while the flat top provides space for stacked towels and baskets of bath supplies. Opt for blue green or true blue for a traditional country look.

real country

Projects crafted for a country bathroom are more authentic with a handmade look, so try new techniques and finishes to personalize a dated space.

check mates

Weatherproof deck paint is a wise choice for a bathroom floor. Impervious to moisture, it comes in a wide range of colors.

HOW TO
paint a checkered floor

1. **Clean** the floor with trisodium phosphate (TSP) cleaner to remove grease and grime. Sand with 220-grit sandpaper to dull the shine. Wipe clean, and apply a liquid deglosser for better paint adhesion.
2. **Paint** the lightest color of latex paint, covering the floor completely. Add a second coat if necessary. Let dry for several days.
3. **Mark** the checkerboard pattern on the floor. Working with a partner, make marks along the
4. wall edges to indicate the size of the checked pattern, and then pull a string from side to side. Tape the string in place; mark along the string
5. with colored pencils close in tone to the darker paint color. Repeat the process to create both sides of the checks.
   Edge the squares using painter's tape. Burnish the edges of the tape to keep paint from seeping under the tape.
   Apply paint using a small roller, *below right*. Add a second coat if necessary. Remove the tape; let paint dry.
6. **Protect** the painted floor with two coats of polyurethane, sanding lightly between coats and picking up dust with a tack cloth.

pot it up

A sunny bathroom windowsill offers the best growing environment—sun and moisture—for a collection of herbs, *left*. Pot them in favorite ceramic pieces, such as these cream-color McCoy pots. Snip the plants back every month or so to keep them from becoming too leggy.

fill it up

Gather flowers from your garden for bathroom bouquets, *right*. Tulips in rosy shades fill a classic compote to overflowing. For a small bouquet, pick a small container in a simple shape and pack it with one variety of blooms.

shake it up

These vintage sugar shakers and salt shakers may be a little rusty, *left*, but they still have some life left in them. Just think of them as diminutive glass vases with built-in flower frogs. Enlarge the shaker holes with an awl if necessary. Tuck delicate stems inside, and set them on a ledge or windowsill where they'll catch the light.

store in style

In a bathroom there's need for storage around every corner. Here's where to find it in a fresh country-style space.

safe storage

Extra floor space in a country bathroom makes room for furniture, such as this pie safe used to store towels, toilet paper, and shampoo. Choose wisely so the piece can keep clutter away. Look for old cupboards with doors that hide a mess behind a classic country pattern.

little splashes

▐ Looking for free help? Get advice on hanging shelves and towel bars or learn painting techniques and wallpapering tips at a home center or hardware store.

open storage

An edited collection of bath accessories adds just the right country flavor when put on display. Search for a towel rack like this one made from tree branches, fill an old basket with towels, and set favorite items on a rustic shelf. Look for distinctive pieces that make everyday items worthy of display.

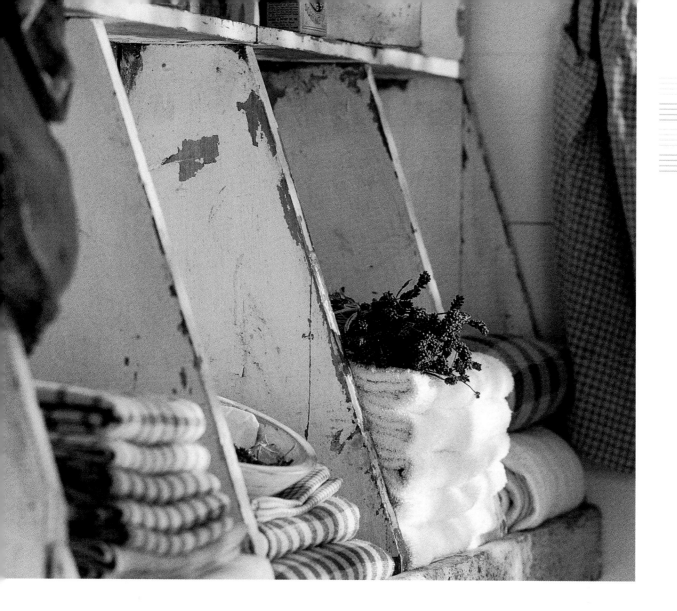

bin storage

Vintage pieces not meant for the bathroom may gain new-fashioned usefulness. These antique bins from a turn-of-the-century hardware store offer open storage that's sized for stacks of towels. If the paint finish starts flaking, seal the bins with two coats of polyurethane.

rake rack

A few alterations turn this outdoor rake into a unique towel rack. To make the rack, cut the rake handle to a shorter length and drill a hole through the end of the handle. Hang the rake from a hook on the wall or from a peg rack. To keep the rake looking its best, seal the wood surface with two coats of polyurethane. Sand lightly between coats.

hang it right

Hooks, loops, and pegs top any window with style.

mighty hooks

Give tab-top curtains modern appeal by suspending them from brushed-steel door hooks screwed to the top of the window frame. Space the hooks to allow room for the curtain to drape. Shop at a home center for hooks that each cost $3 or less for the most economical solution.

top knots

Already fitted with grommets for hanging, shower curtains are a clever no-sew window treatment. Purchase a standard 8-foot shower rod at a home center and coat it with a coordinating paint color. Slip a length of ribbon through each grommet, and tie the ribbon to a drapery rod. Voilà!

shaker pegs

Look for Shaker pegs in the dowel section of a home center. Drill ⅜-inch-deep holes in the window frame. Space the holes 6 inches apart. Cover the end of each peg with wood glue; slip it into a predrilled hole and let dry. Purchase a curtain or valance with tie tops, or add ties to a purchased curtain. For a no-sew option, use ribbon as ties.

hammer heads

There's truth in the country adage that the simplest solution can be the best. Here, rosehead nails provide the hardware for hanging curtains. Just tap them into place using a hammer. At pennies each, the nails are affordable, too. Look for these nails at online sites that offer old-fashioned products.

stick pins

Here's an easy way to hang a flat panel: Use stick pins. Look for them at stores that carry drapery items and window hardware. Purchase a lace panel that's slightly larger than the window frame. At the top, push a pin through each corner of the panel and into the window frame. Sweep a bottom corner to the window sash on the opposite side and pin it to the frame. That's an installation time of 5 minutes or less.

kids

Kids just want to have fun, so decorate their bathrooms

in a playful style that's also waterproof.

Combine colorful walls, whimsical patterns,

and easy-care finishes for a look that's

kid-proof and parent-friendly.

Add accessories such as baskets, shelves,

and pockets that make it easy for kids

to keep the bathroom neat and tidy.

rub a dub

just ducky

It's only paint, right? So layer on the fun with stripes and stencils that turn anyone into an artist.

5 ideas under $100

① Pick a color scheme of blue and yellow, but don't limit yourself to pastels. Mid-range or bold shades of these two colors add a style wallop that any kid will love. Look at the mid- to dark tones on a color card for the best choices. Use primer tinted close to the blue for the best paint coverage. White fixtures and floors promise to balance any strong colors.

② Plain walls can be boring. Give them some pizzazz by dividing and conquering. Use a carpenter's level and a pencil to mark a horizontal line 36 to 40 inches from the floor. For marks that disappear as the paint is applied, use colored pencils. The height of the sink can also provide a guideline because the border should clear the top of the sink.

③ Vary the techniques in a room that's all about paint. A color-washed top wall sidles up to a wordy border. To create a color-washed wall, use a wide brush to apply glaze in a cross-hatch motion. Stripes on the bottom wall add a graphic note. Pencil the location of the stripes but don't add painter's tape. Simply brush glaze along the penciled marks to create a soft edge. A row of stenciled ducks stair-steps around the room.

④ Furniture that's functional is the only choice for a bathroom for kids. The narrow stand slips into a corner of the bathroom and keeps bathing supplies where kids can reach them. Extra features, such as metal bins or woven baskets, store and serve as portable carriers. Paint an outdoor bench green to serve as a handy perch for towels or for drying off a child after a bath.

⑤ Patches of solid color ground busy walls, so add plain window shades, bath mats, and towels.

little splashes

▌ Add towel storage by installing three towel bars on the back of the bathroom door. The lower bars are just the right height for kids.

juvenile edition

A bathroom for the whole family can sport a young look.
Here's how to clean up with a playful attitude.

5 ideas under $100

① Give boring walls a little architectural interest by adding wainscoting made from 1x2s applied vertically and topped with a horizontal 1x3. Apply the boards directly to drywall or plaster using nails or screws. Add a second 1x3 as a useful and groovy shelf by gluing and nailing it to the wall and to the other 1x3. Paint walls and trim in a playful shade. Look for paints treated with mildewcide to eliminate worries about mildew.

② A top sheet makes a good shower curtain. To add fun-loving spirit, choose sheets made for kids or teens that feature bright colors, bold patterns, and interesting ruffled cuffs. (Buy pillowcases, too, and use them as window valances.) Wash the sheet to preshrink the fabric. Add grommets along one side of the sheet so the top edge of the sheet serves as the curtain's vertical border. It's easy to add grommets; just follow the package instructions. Hem the bottom edge so the shower curtain hangs a few inches above the floor.

③ Look for hardware that does double duty. This double towel bar multiplies the hanging space so each child has his or her own spot for towels. Make sure you allow one bar per child. Looking for options? Type "towel bar" into an Internet search engine. Make sure towel bars are anchored into the walls. For wall anchors suitable for the wall materials, check at the home center or hardware store.

④ Kids will take care of their stuff if they have a handy place to put it. Try this idea: Label mesh makeup bags with key-chain tags outfitted with each child's picture. Store toothpaste and a toothbrush in each bag. When things get messy, empty the mesh bags and drop them into the washing machine.

⑤ Add a moisture-friendly window treatment when the window is adjacent to the tub. A rattan blind shrugs off humidity or splashes without obscuring the view when the lights are on. For privacy night and day, use patterned or translucent window film over the glass panes on the lower half of the window. Look for static-cling films that are easy to remove and replace.

little splashes

▌ Children's coloring books offer inspiration for custom stencils. The simple shapes in the books transfer to walls with ease.

just a little splashier

Playing is job #1 for kids, so make sure their bathrooms are an environment filled with fun and color.

get the look

▌ Pick a gender-neutral color scheme when boys and girls use the same bathroom. Feel free to choose saturated colors because a bathroom is small and separated from other rooms. Elements such as white fixtures and tile will naturally balance bold colors.

▌ Shop for durability. Semigloss paints are easier to scrub than matte paints. Cotton fabrics wear well and promise easy care. Consider outdoor fabrics and rugs that shed water; they also eliminate a surface for mold to grow.

▌ Add kid-friendly storage. Shelves, baskets, and towel bars at kid-height as well as handy mesh bags and wall-hung totes eliminate excuses for leaving a bathroom messy.

▌ Build in flexibility so it's easy to change the bath as kids grow up. Add borders of wallpaper or stencils that can be removed and replaced. Painted designs that require expertise and a lot of time should be considered permanent.

▌ Be ready for a quick change. A bathroom used by kids takes a beating. Stockpile an extra shower curtain, towels, or rugs when they're deeply discounted. Stay tuned into sales by signing up for e-mails from favorite catalog retailers. When the bath looks trashed, bring out a fresh look.

▌ Plan for safety. Add no-slip decals to the tub bottom, replace glass bottles and glasses with plastic, place a spongy cover-up on the tub faucet, and provide a step stool for access to the sink.

Hooks Never leave doubt about whose towel is clean and ready for action. Give each child a hook attached to a letter of the alphabet. Look for pre-made letter hooks, or create one by stenciling a letter on an oval plaque and attaching a hook to the plaque's bottom edge.

Decals Easy up and easy off, decals offer a quick way to change a kid's bathroom as their interests change. Look for versions that attach to porcelain, acrylic, mirrors, and cabinetry and come off without damaging the surface.

Rugs Provide a soft landing spot by the tub with a rug that fits the scheme. Look for bright colors, soft texture, and washability.

Stencils Wake up bathroom walls with an overscaled stencil. Forget sweet and small. Look for a pattern to wrap around the ceiling or to add at wainscot height. Look for stencil companies that offer one pattern in several sizes.

Waste can Even the trash adds to the decor when it's hidden away in a hot-pink trashcan with a pop-up lid. Go for a bold color, and think in multiples. After all, lidded cans are perfect for storage too.

Shower curtains A new shower curtain is the fastest way to freshen a stale bath. When it comes to a child's bathroom, select a shower curtain that reflects his or her current interests or tastes.

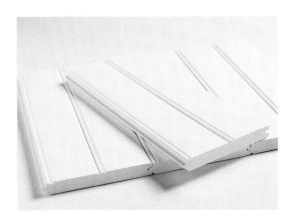

Beaded board This classic material is perfect for use in small, affordable doses. Add it to cabinet doors, use it as a backing for a peg rack, or wrap it as a wide border around a mirror.

project time

Let the kids help create these bathroom projects or assist with picking colors and designs—with supervision, of course.

stamp style

A whimsical stamped design hides dated vinyl flooring under a room-freshening coat of paint. Outdated vinyl flooring in good shape is a prime candidate for painting. If the floor is worn or flaking, however, paint will only emphasize the problems.

HOW TO
paint and stamp a vinyl floor

1. **Choose** a rubber stamp that accommodates both the shape and design of the vinyl flooring. Flat- or pebble-surfaced vinyl floors can handle almost any stamped design. Keep in mind that hard-surface vinyls accept paint better than softer types. Use only flexible water-base paints on cushiony vinyl flooring.

2. **Remove** any wax and thoroughly clean the vinyl flooring with TSP (trisodium phosphate) to ensure that the paint sticks. Then apply a liquid sanding solution to prepare the surface.

3. **Prime** the vinyl. Use a roller and an extension handle to apply the primer while standing. Apply two coats if necessary.

4. **Roll** on two coats of floor paint. Floor paint withstands traffic, suits many types of floors, and works indoors and outdoors.

5. **Practice** the stamped design on a sample board. Roll an accent paint color onto a stamp; apply to the sample. Try blotting the stamp before applying it to the surface, *below left*. Once the look is right, apply the stamp randomly across the floor. Recoat the stamp with paint as necessary.

6. **Protect** the floor finish with two coats of water-base polyurethane.

sweet finish

A simple fabric skirt around the sink hides storage boxes or a step stool for little ones. Fabric gathered into soft folds is applied to the underside of the sink base with hook-and-loop tape; it easily removes for laundering. Affordable outdoor lanterns are an unexpected alternative to expensive wall sconces that stand up to bathroom humidity.

little splashes

▌If several children share one bathroom, let each child pick a favorite paint color from a pre-selected group. Buy a quart of each color; apply as bold color blocks on the walls.

stash-away curtain

Create a handy shower stash with this simple sewing project. Create a shower liner from athletic mesh and fit it with pockets to hold lightweight bath gear. Elastic slipped through a fabric casing makes a gathered top to keep pockets from spilling the goods. After a good soak, bath-time toys drain right into the tub.

his or hers

Colors rather than details make these bathroom vanities and mirrors just right for a boy or girl.

all-american boy

Bring on the red, white, and blue to create a perfectly patriotic boy's bathroom. The look is easy to achieve in a basic bathroom, and best of all, it works for boys of all ages. Start by painting a vanity cabinet blue. After letting the topcoat dry, distress the surface with sandpaper. That's a guaranteed way to help new dings and dents blend in.

Create a focal-point mirror by adding a frame of wide boards around an existing mirror. Divide the surface into playful and colorful stars and stripes. After painting the frame, distress it with sandpaper. Accessories, such as striped towels in patriotic colors and old jars filled with toothbrushes and cotton swabs, carry out the theme.

totally girly

Sugar and spice is totally nice for a girl's bathroom. Soft pastels provide the sugar while a wash of wood stain adds the spice. To create this look, start with a basic vanity and brush it with a coat of off-white paint. To age it even more, sand the surface and wipe it with a dark stain. Wipe off some of the stain, but leave some behind to highlight the vanity's details. New crystal knobs add the right girly touch. Replace the mirror with a frame made of beaded board and edged with wood banding. Paint the beaded board in a range of favorite colors, sand lightly, cut to length, and nail to a plywood backing. Glue the mirror to the center of the plywood, and cover the inner and outer edges with wood banding. Change the accessories to suit the age and interests of the occupant.

index

American flag motif, 124
Antique style, *See also* Flea market style, 10–11
Artwork, 29, 30–31, 88

Bamboo, used as cabinet insert, 24
Baskets, 81, 102, 105
Bath mats, diamond cut-out
    project, 60
Bathtubs
    clawfoot, 79, 102, 103
    covering, 47
    framed prints around, 30, 31
    framing of, 12, 13
Beach style, 86–99
    accessories, 88, 91, 92–97, 99
    color schemes, 92
    ideas/themes for, 88–91
    storage, 110–11
    tips, 92
Beaded board, 8, 93, 105, 121
Benches, 116
Black, use of, 39
Blinds, 76
Bottle garden, 33

Cabinets, *See also* Vanities, 8, 11, 21, 24, 84
Candelabras, 93
Candles, 29
Caulk, 45
Cedar planking, 24
Ceramic wall and floor tile
    covering with exterior siding, 67
    embossed pieces, 43
    on focal point wall, 91
    incorporation of vintage, 11, 36
    painting of, 91
    use based on size of space, 14
    white, 64
Chairs, 11, 12, 43, 79, 81, 83, 84
Chair slipcover, 83
Chandeliers, 14, 15, 88
Classic style, 34–47
    accessories, 36, 40, 42, 43
    color schemes, 42
    fabric, 46–47
    ideas/themes for, 36–40
    tips, 42
    wall treatments, 44–45
Collections, display of, 67, 68, 73
Color schemes
    beach, 92
    classic, 42
    country, 105, 106
    flea market, 64, 68
    kid-friendly, 116, 120
    nature-inspired, 24, 27, 28
    neutral, 8, 40
    red and white, 38–39
    romantic, 8, 14
    selection of, 27
    spa, 76, 80
    whimsical, 50, 54
Country style, 100–113
    accessories, 102, 105, 106–107
    color schemes, 105, 106
    floor treatment, 108
    ideas/themes for, 102–105
    storage, 110–111
    tips, 106
    window treatments, 112–115
Crystal-embellished lamp shade, 18
Curtains. *See* Window treatments

Daisy motif, 52–53
Decals, 120
Decoupage treatment, 12
Dimmer switches, 17, 80
Dressers, 20, 99, 102, 105
Dressing table, 46
Duck motif, 116–117

Etched mirrors, 16
Etched vases, 95

Fabric. *See also* Shower curtains; Window treatments
    bathtub coverup, 47
    blue ticking, 107
    dressing table, 46
    floral pattern, 67
    mixing patterns, 64
    outdoor fabrics, 54
    retail sources, 54
    skirts around sinks, 11, 36, 40, 64, 123
    tablecloths as, 69
    tropical pattern, 64
    washability test, 12
Face scrub, 83
Flea market style, 62–73
    accessories, 64, 69, 72–73
    color schemes, 64, 68
    ideas/themes for, 64–67
    paint treatments, 70
    tips, 68
    window treatments, 67, 71
Floor cloths. *See* Rugs and floor cloths
Floors. *See also* Ceramic wall and floor tile
    lace stencil treatment, 19
    painting, 19, 29, 108, 122
    stamp treatment on vinyl
        flooring, 122
    vinyl floor tiles, 67, 76
Flowerpots, 69, 109
Flowers, 27, 55, 76, 109
Focal points, 42, 68, 92
Frames, 30, 68
French style, 12–13

Glass accessories, 69, 92, 97
Glass mosaic tiles, 88, 92

Herbal bouquets, 80

Jewelry, as artwork, 40

Kids' bathrooms, 114–125
    accessories, 124, 125
    color schemes, 116, 120
    ideas/themes for, 116–119
    tips, 120

Ladders, 12, 25
Letters, 36, 84, 120
Lights and lighting
    chandeliers, 14, 15, 88
    covers for fluorescent
        fixtures, 36
    dimmer switches, 17, 80
    embellished shades, 11, 18
    painting of, 8, 11
    sconces, 42, 50, 91
    upgrade for more light, 42

Mirrors
    American flag frame, 124
    collections of, 72
    displayed with oversized
        letters, *36*
    etchings on, 16
    gold, 14, 43
    hanging techniques, 17
    molding around, 8
    mosaic embellishment, 98
    from old windows, 40
    paint embellishment, 50, 55
    rustic, 24
    shell embellishment, 91, 98, 99
    striped frame for, 57
Monograms, 88
Murals, 30

Nature-inspired style, 22–33
  accessories, 24, 29, 33
  artwork, 29, 30–31
  color schemes, 24, 27, 28
  fern floor cloth, 32
  ideas/themes for, 24–27
  tips, 28
Neutral color schemes, 8, 40

Paint and painting. *See also* Color schemes
  color washing treatment, 116
  dressers, 20
  faux wood finish, 76
  floors, 19, 29, 108, 122
  light fixtures, 8, 11
  milk paint for vintage finish, 102
  mirrors, 50, 55
  shower curtains, 61
  stamp treatment, 58–59, 122
  stencil treatment, 19, 44, 53, 116, 119, 121
  stripes, 24, 45, 70, 116
  tile, 91
  window treatments, 58–59
  wood knobs, 53
Paneling, 27, 102
Paper lanterns, 55
Peg rack, 43, 85
Photographs, 30, 97
Pie safe, 110
Plants, 28, 33, 109
Plaster stencils, 44
Plates, 11, 40, 67, 69, 73
Polka dots, 50–51, 59

Red-and-white color scheme, 38–39
Roman shades, 67, 79
Romantic style, 6–21
  accessories, 15
  color schemes, 8, 14
  dressers, 20
  ideas/themes for, 8–13
  lace floor treatment, 19
  lights and lighting, 14, 15, 18
  tips, 14
Rugs and floor cloths
  from bath mats, 27
  braided rugs, 106
  fern floor cloth, 32
  flower rug project, 53
  herringbone floor cloth, 82
  selection of, 27
  sources for vintage, 8
  striped floor cloth, 56
  sun-fading, 8
  toile floor cloth, 39
Rustic style, 27

Salt and pepper shakers, 109
Sconces, 42, 50, 91
Shades, lamp, 11, 18
Shades, window, 58–59, 67, 76, 79, 89
Shells, 88, 91, 92–93, 96, 98, 99
Shelves
  around room, 27, 40
  brackets, 15, 107
  chrome-painted, 15
  at head of tub, 93
  installation tips, 12
  open floor units, 39
  overhead, 67
  scalloped, 94
Shower curtains
  from bath sheets, 50
  from bed sheets, 55, 119
  from curtain panels, 64
  extra-tall, 105
  mesh storage liner, 123
  as window treatments, 112
  words added to, 61

Showerheads, 29, 81
Shutters, 36
Siding, 67
Sinks
  pedestal style, 24, 91
  skirts around, 11, 36, 40, 64, 123
  washbasins, 69
Small rooms, 40, 67, 91
Soaps, 80
Spa style, 74–85
  accessories, 76, 79, 81, 82–83
  color schemes, 76, 79–80
  elements in, 80–81
  herringbone floor cloth, 82
  ideas/themes for, 76–79
  storage, 84–85
  tips, 80
Spa trays, 81, 85
Stamp treatment, 58–59, 122
Stencil treatment, 19, 44, 53, 116, 119, 121
Stone accessories, 24
Storage boxes, 15

Tablecloths, 69, 71
Tables, 53, 80, 84
Texture, use of, 14, 28, 42, 80, 92
Ticking, 107
Tile, ceramic. *See* Ceramic wall and floor tile
Tile, vinyl floor, 67, 76
Toile, 37, 39
Towel bars and racks, 43, 71, 111, 116, 119, 120
Towels
  embellishments, 50, 81
  monograms, 88
  storage ideas, 11, 12, 24, 85, 106, 110–111, 116, 119, 120
Tropical style, 64–65

Valances, 53, 71, 95
Vanities
  customization of basic, 98, 124–125
  decoupage treatment, 12
  faux wood finish, 76
  hardware for, 14, 53
  kid-friendly, 124–125
  pine tables as, 102
Vases, 55, 95, 109
Vinyl flooring, stamp treatment, 122
Vinyl floor tiles, 67, 76

Wainscots, 102, 105, 119
Wallpaper, 11, 12, 27, 42, 68, 76
Wall treatments. *See also* Ceramic
  wall and floor tile;
  Paint and painting
  adhesive letters, 85
  beaded board, 8, 93, 105, 121
  exterior siding, 67
  plaster stencils, 44
Wastecans, 121
Whimsical style, 48–61
  accessories, 55, 56–57, 60–61
  color schemes, 50, 54
  ideas/themes for, 50–53
  tips, 54
  window treatments, 58–59
Windowsill displays, 67, 109
Window treatments
  blinds, 76
  embellishments, 58–59
  grommets, 50
  hardware, 112–113
  moisture-friendly, 119
  painting, 58–59
  privacy window films, 79, 119
  shades, 58–59, 67, 76, 79, 89
  shell swag, 96
  shutters, 36
  valances, 53, 71, 95

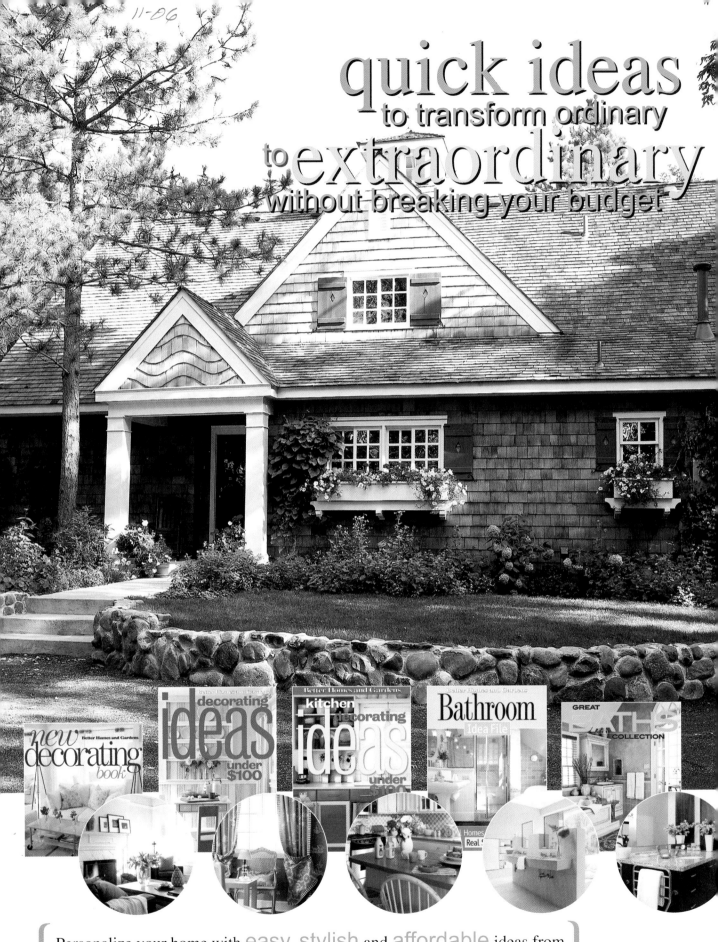

quick ideas
to transform ordinary
to extraordinary
without breaking your budget

{ Personalize your home with easy, stylish and affordable ideas from a source you trust. Found wherever home improvement books are sold. }